HOW
SHOULD
A BODY
BE?

HOW SHOULD A BODY BE?

A MEMOIR

BETHANY MELOCHE

To my husband—
I love you.

♥

CONTENTS

PROLOGUE

"Do you want anything to eat?" asked one of my bridesmaids.

"No, thanks," I said, staring at my reflection in a hand-held mirror.

"You should really eat something," chimed in bridesmaid #2.

"How about a muffin?" It was bridesmaid #3 this time.

"Not until the dress is zipped up," I said, waving them off without looking in any of their three directions.

A muffin magically appeared a few minutes later.

The dress was successfully zipped up shortly after (with the help of two assistants, a lot of sucking in, and some grunts from all involved), and the muffin may or may not have been eaten shortly after that. I could read between the lines—or in this case, the grunts and scoffs—that my loved ones didn't know why I couldn't eat a muffin or why I had to order my dress in the smallest size possible. Maybe because it was out of character for me to be so image conscious—me, who never wore a dab of makeup, but for this day had spent an hour at Sephora identifying the perfect shade of lipstick. (It was still too peachy, not enough pink.)

Self-consciously I wondered if they thought I was being extra silly because my body was obviously, irredeemably, permanently imperfect.

But maybe that was the reason for my fixation on looking beautiful, and on this particular day.

I went through life with a body that the world told me was not how a body should be (and people really did tell me this, to my face), and so there was part of me that thought, maybe magically, that maybe on this day—just this *one* day—that if everything were perfect, we could all pretend otherwise.

I could feel otherwise.

Everything was seemingly perfect, though I couldn't help but recoil when the photographer took shots of my Maid of Honor putting on my wedding shoes. I let him snap away, even as I knew none of those photos would make it into the album. To look underneath my dress was to destroy the illusion that I was like any other picture-perfect bride—that I had the body a bride was supposed to have.

I had to hope that on this day the world would not whisper about the way I walked down the aisle or what lay underneath those layers of satin and tulle. That instead they would see what I did when I caught my reflection again in the mirror.

1

DIAGNOSIS

I peered up the stairs from the living room, keeping the rest of my body hidden behind the bland white wall detailed with the perfectly eighties mauve trim my mother loved. My dad was upstairs in his office working, and I could see my mom in the kitchen, busily chatting with a friend—covering topics like what had happened at last week's prayer group, her struggle to find the perfect rhyming couplet for her latest children's book, and what a shame it is that Sally's kids are back in rehab. *Perfect.* I really didn't want my parents to know what I was up to. I needed to ensure privacy, silence, focus.

Satisfied with my inspection, I returned to my favorite spot in our house: the computer station. It was 2004 and our family shared a clunky desktop PC, all beige housing and blocky design. I sat at the worn wooden desk (bought by my mom at a garage sale) that was nestled in the corner of our living room, but still purposefully situated in such a way that the screen was in full view if my parents decided to come down the stairs. The computer station felt more like an afterthought to the layout, stuck behind our large couches which, contrarily, were laid out like kings in front of our big central TV. To me, the computer had always been the most interesting thing in the room. The computer was my connection from our suburban Michigan home to the outside world, and I was convinced that anything I wanted to know could be obtained from the depths of the web. In the early 2000s the internet was full of arts and crafts ideas, sites that let me take care of tiny virtual pets, and chats with strangers on AIM. Based on the way that I chattered about the pixelated chihuahua I had successfully kept alive for three days, or the Shrinky Dink instructions I had stumbled across, my dad had promised me that for my thirteenth birthday—next month!—I would get my own computer. Until then I had to make do with a shared one. A public one. One in full view.

This wasn't ideal for my project, but it would have to do. The situation was urgent.

I swiveled in the standard black computer chair, clicking the Internet Explorer icon repeatedly in the hopes that that would make it come up faster. I always felt that it did.

Finally, Explorer—and the home page: Google.

I typed my queries into the search bar, my fingers shaking from a combination of speed, excitement, and terror.

nerve pain
lightning feeling in arm
how do you know you have nerve disease
inherited disease tooth

I didn't slow down long enough to read the pages of results that came up; I knew what I was looking for, and what to do once I found it.

Because this time, I wasn't just looking around. I was looking for an answer.

Earlier that day, I had been playing with my best friend Leslie on her living room floor. Leslie was four months older than me and had already turned thirteen, but I had maintained a solid inch over her in height, so I felt like I still had the competitive edge. Leslie and I loved crafts and creating something out of nothing. Today we were creating a line of baked goods, except we didn't use flour, sugar, butter; we used clay. Over the years Leslie and I had spent playing, I had learned how to make colorful miniatures out of clay, and my specialty was tiny food items. I could spend an hour crafting one perfect little doughnut, placing each individual nearly microscopic rainbow-colored sprinkle on its frosted topping. I could sculpt smaller items and in greater detail than anyone I knew, and I took my role as both sculptor and master (clay) baker seriously. On this day I was teaching Leslie how to weave the delicate pattern for a pie crust.

Leslie was working on the crust and I was busy making tiny stemless cherries to fill the pie with, when I felt what I imagined lightning would feel like if it hit your skin. A shock traveled down the entire length of my right arm, from shoulder to wrist, in an instant. I looked down for a spider, or a stick pin, something that would explain why my arm hurt. But all I could see was my light tan arm, the blue sleeve of my t-shirt, the smoothness of my skin, the pin-sized birthmarks that had been there since I was born. This had to be coming from inside. The pain was sharp, almost prickly. And then, just as suddenly as it had arrived, it was gone. I looked over at Leslie sitting across from me. She was still intently weaving together strips of beige clay, unaware of the fact that once-in-a-lifetime (or so I thought) lightning had struck. I looked down at my arm as if I didn't know whose it was anymore. I touched it with just the tip of my finger, sensing that it was a stranger's. But my arm looked just fine, as if the lightning had never happened.

I felt the pain—had I injured myself somehow?—once more while we finished making our pie, just for it to be gone again in a flash. But as much as the front of my brain brushed it off, a tiny part of me knew, even though the pain was gone, that it was significant. As I'd grown up, I had occasionally heard my dad's family discuss me in strange, hushed tones. Every so often, I overheard my mom say my name while on the phone with my grandmother, her mother-in-law. One time, she said something really weird. It sounded like, "Was it the tooth?"

Later, I confronted my mother and asked her why she was talking about my teeth. I found myself unconsciously running my tongue over them to make sure they weren't crooked, and they weren't. So what could be wrong with them? Or maybe so right? "It's a nerve problem in your dad's family," she said. "It's called CMT—the T stands for 'tooth'."

"Are you worried I have it?"

"No, honey. Remember we checked you out when you were nine—you're good."

Now I remembered visiting my primary care doctor, who'd asked me to walk down the hall for him. "She's fine," he'd said to my mom after I'd smoothly walked to the end and back. His visual diagnosis was good enough for me, good enough for her, and good enough for my body.

But when we drove home from Leslie's house, I remembered that conversation with my mom. I remembered the appointment. Maybe something *was* wrong with my nerves, maybe that was the source of the lightning in my arm.

Maybe the doctor had been wrong.

age you get CMT
does CMT hurt
chance of getting CMT from your dad
how to know if you have CMT
CMT diagnosis

I'd found enough. I heard my mother's footsteps heading down the stairs, and raced to close the browser, quickly, as if I were hiding explicit material. (I guess, in a way, that I was?) My mission had been a success; I had found the answers I was looking for. They were enough to present my findings to my father.

I approached him when he came downstairs to watch TV. During a commercial break, I sidled up next to him on one of our mauve couches.

"What's up, Pooh?" he said.

Pooh Bear, or Pooh for short, was his favorite nickname for me. Even though "Pooh" usually got some snickers when he used it in public, I let it go. I liked being Pooh.

I didn't waste any time on chit-chat.

"Dad, I think I might have CMT."

He was quiet. My dad always said that some people think to talk, and some people talk to think. He and my mom both agreed that he was in the former camp, she in the latter.

He didn't look at me, but my dad was never a fan of eye contact; that on top of his often slow response time meant that it was always a challenge to know whether he was even listening to you at all, or solving other, more *interesting* problems in his head: revolutionizing software development, writing catchy direct marketing headlines, figuring out where Mom hid the Oreos. Finally he spoke. "Oh, Pooh. Ask your mom to make an appointment with a neurologist."

What? That was it? I was all ready and anxious to share my research and my findings on neuropathy and nerve degeneration and nerve pain, but he didn't ask for any of my evidence. I was disappointed to not have the opportunity to show off my expansive knowledge, but I knew there would be other opportunities.

I told my mom what Dad had said. I heard her confer with my grandmother on the phone later that day, though I couldn't pick up the details, and then, just like that, an appointment was scheduled.

A few weeks later, when my parents and I walked into the clinic, I was filled with excitement. I was ready to receive my diagnosis. I felt fully confident that I would be getting an answer that very day (with scores of treatment options unfurling before me), and besides, lucky for the neurologist, I had already done all of the hard work for him. But even though I was sure I had figured out what was wrong with me, I wanted it made official. I wanted a piece of paper that said "you have *this*." I wanted the validation that I'd been looking for the last five years because those lightning bolts weren't the first thing to go wrong (and I'll get to those other things, later). I wanted the certainty that yes, there was something going on inside me. That something was wrong, and it had a name. (And maybe, even, something that could help?)

A nurse led us into a large room with over a dozen lightly-cushioned examination beds lining its perimeter, each beside a curtain attached to the ceiling that could be pulled around it for privacy. My head was immediately filled with the sounds of curtains whirring back and forth, murmured conversations, and of hurried steps of nurses and clinicians darting back and forth between patients. I heard the same phrase over and over again: "Hi there, I'm Dr. ____. What brings you in today?"

It doesn't always take an outwardly dramatic event for there to be a massive—and meaningful—shift in who you are, and how you relate to your body. Sometimes it can be as simple as walking into a room. When you walk back out, you may not yet know that a change has taken place—but in time you find yourself realizing that the person you were upon entering is fundamentally different than the person you left as. You start referring to yourself and who you are as pre-event and post-event, or pre-room and post-room. In my case, it was pre-diagnosis and post-diagnosis. When you look back on an unrelated event, you may think "that was before." Now, when you meet a new friend, for example, you know that they will only ever know the you that is post-event, post-room, post-diagnosis.

They will never know who you were before.

You can never go back to the you that you were before.

And then, one day, years later, even you will come to forget who you were before.

Susan Sontag writes about the kingdom of the ill, about the moment of crossing over. This room, this bed, these curtains—they were all part of my crossing. At twelve years old, I was ushered into my own Kingdom of the Neurologically Diseased—a place so many of my ancestors before me had entered and left—forever changed.

The nurse led us over to a scale positioned in the center of the room and told me to stand on it. I didn't know what my weight had to do with my arm pain, but I stepped on the scale anyway. I could feel nervous energy coming off of my mom. I could sense that she didn't like me being weighed. As I stepped on, she whispered, "If you don't like it, you don't have to." I told her that it was okay, that I didn't mind. When she repeated herself, I started wondering if I *should* mind. Maybe it was bad for someone to know what I weighed. Or maybe she saw something about me—or my weight—that I couldn't.

The scale read 118, which seemed reasonable to me. I was 5'2—average height for this weight. Phew. I was still standing on the scale when a man in a long white coat walked up next to me. He peered at the number on the scale and said, "Wow, you don't look like you're that heavy!"

What did that mean? His comment annoyed me. Had I been going around thinking I was totally normal but I wasn't? Did other people think I was "that heavy?" I searched my mom's face for signs of equal annoyance, but before I could make eye contact with her, the man in the white coat ushered us toward one of the examination beds.

We took the three chairs by the bed and sat. To my displeasure, the man in the white coat didn't leave. Instead, he introduced himself, shaking both my parents' hands but not offering a hand to me. "I'm Dr. Niro. What brings you in today?"

Great, I thought, *this is the doctor.*

I knew that Dr. Niro was the neurologist my grandma had recommended. So far, he hadn't made a favorable impression on me.

Dr. Niro pulled up a stool on wheels and sat in front of us, his submissive audience. I studied his face; he had richly tanned skin, a strong nose, and a bald head with the exception of some dark hair along the sides, speckled with grey. He looked bored and businesslike.

"So," he repeated, "what brings you in today?"

He said "you" but looked only toward my parents, not me. I was used to this: doctors not taking me seriously because I was only a kid.

"*I* had an episode of nerve pain in my arm," I said. I hoped he caught the stress on the word "I." I. Me. *The patient.*

He turned towards me, and I told Dr. Niro about the lightning bolt in my arm; about how I'd been researching nerve pain and CMT online, and thought there might be a connection.

Dr. Niro scribbled on his clipboard but didn't speak, just nodded and murmured unintelligibly as I gave my spiel.

My dad spoke up. "We have a family history of CMT."

My mom was always the one to take me to my doctor appointments, so I was surprised that morning when my father—who never spoke about CMT—wordlessly got in the car with us.

We all looked over at my dad, and he continued. "My mom has it," he said. "I haven't been tested, but I assume I have it." He spoke as if he were talking about something even less exciting and monumental than the weather.

Dr. Niro gave my dad a weird look that I couldn't interpret, said "Okay," and turned back toward me. "Can you take off your shoes?"

I slowly slipped off my sandals. My Googling of CMT had resulted in some photos of patients' feet. Most of them had high arches like mine, but some of them looked really wonky—curled and contorted, covered with blistering sores. My feet looked nothing like those. They were creamy white, delicate, with straight toes and zero blisters. I half-expected Dr. Niro to take one look at my feet and, with delight, exclaim that they were lovely, that CMT certainly wasn't the issue.

Instead, he rolled his stool closer to me and asked me to lift up my right leg. He took my foot into his hands and manipulated it. He moved it up, down, left, right, and around in circles. His hands were large and strong with patches of black hair, and the hands of a stranger on my feet felt strangely intimate. Especially knowing that those hands were searching for hidden signs of disease. Knowing that they could feel things that I couldn't, even though I'd been living with my feet for twelve years and he'd only touched them for twelve seconds. That they could recognize clues, hidden deep beneath the surface of my skin.

I wondered what he was thinking about my feet. Did they smell? Did they look weirder than I knew? He slid a hand underneath my forefoot. "Push against my hand."

I pushed as hard as I could, trying to point my foot.

"Good, good," he said.

This approving word made me feel good. This meant that the doctor thought I was strong and that I could follow basic instructions.

He moved his hand so that it was resting on top of my forefoot. "Now the other way; try to pull your toes up."

I tried. My foot didn't move. At all. *Huh, that's odd. Is it supposed to move? It must be if he's asking—*

"Try to pull your toes up," he said again. His voice was louder this time.

"I am!" I replied. I didn't like the helplessness in my voice.

He didn't say anything, just made a "Hmmmmmm" noise. *What did that mean? Had I failed?* I was about to ask to try again when he let go of my foot and let my leg fall to the ground.

"Let me see your hands."

I held them out in front of me. He took hold of them one by one and examined them—for what, I wasn't sure. I liked my hands; they were small with smooth pale skin, and could craft a cherry pie the size of a quarter. I hadn't ever thought anything was wrong with them. Sure, my arm might be full of lightning, and my feet seemed strangely disconnected from my brain, but my hands—they'd always been reliable. They let me make tiny cherries; type anything I wanted into my beloved search bar; grab my dad's arm during a particularly scary part of a movie. Stretching out the webbing between my index finger and thumb between his fingers, Dr. Niro straightened my fingers, spinning my thumb in circles like a propellor.

"Squeeze my finger," he said, pointing his index finger. I grabbed his wide finger and squeezed it as hard as I could. I squeezed so hard that my whole body felt drained after I let go. I stared at his face the entire time, and he didn't even flinch. *Was he just acting manly or did he really not feel anything?*

"Now walk for me."

Neurologists sure do get to order people around a lot, I thought.

I stood up, still barefoot, and walked several paces out into the middle of the room. Sure, I had always been clumsy, bumping into things or tripping over my own feet, normal kid stuff, so here I focused on walking as straight and "well" as I could— whatever that meant. I was torn between the part of me that wanted a diagnosis, that was full speed ahead into whatever having CMT could or would mean (and my dad was fine, and my grandma was fine, so it couldn't be that bad?), and the part of me that didn't want to have something visibly wrong with me. It had been one thing to be skulking around my living room, sneakily typing "nerve pain" into the search bar and getting excited about presenting my findings to my father. It was another to be here, in the hospital, where the smells were strong and antiseptic, where I could hear the rustling of other patients, and start to sense that my body was different, in ways I couldn't see. It was one thing, I was coming to realize, to anticipate having something wrong with you. It was quite another to have others see that there actually is.

"Now turn and come back."

I turned around and walked back.

Dr. Niro scribbled more notes on his clipboard, but didn't say anything.

"Stay standing," he said, just as I was about to take a seat.

He got up now and stood right in front of me.

"Now try to stand still."

I had just started to think, *well that isn't so hard*, when he took both palms and *pushed me* hard against my shoulders. I lost my balance and stumbled backwards.

"Try to stay still," he said, and then pushed me again.

And again.

What a jerk.

He got in several pushes, but toward the end I started pushing back with my body weight. I didn't know if he could tell, but I hoped he could sense my subtle aggression.

Satisfied with his pushing me around, Dr. Niro returned to his seat. This was apparently the conclusion of his pointless exam, his grand finale.

He didn't apologize for pushing me. Instead, he spoke to my father now.

"You said a relative has already seen me?" he asked.

"Yes, my mother, May Meloche."

"Well, I can't comment on another patient but I'm going to take a quick look at her chart. Stay here."

With that, Dr. Niro left the room.

As soon as he swept past the curtain, I turned to my parents.

"Can you believe he *pushed* me? He almost made me fall over!"

"That was my favorite part," said my dad, laughing too loudly for an open room. My mom laughed too, though at a more tolerable noise level. I glared at them both—I thought his joke was slightly funny too, but I refused to laugh. One person pushing me around was enough for the day, without this quickly devolving into the Let's Make Fun of Bethany™ show.

We spent the next several minutes waiting in silence until Dr. Niro finally came back with a chart in hand and returned to his seat.

He looked at me this time and said, "Well, you do have CMT."

This is not how I'd pictured any of this. I had imagined, when I had imagined it, that receiving a diagnosis would be more... special. That the doctor would close the door, pull his chair closer, and suddenly speak in a soft, kind voice. He'd tell me not to be scared, that I would get through this. That there were tremendous new treatment options and great strides had been made. That there's a great clinical trial going on out of Johns Hopkins and really, this would be a bump in the road but only make me a stronger, better person.

That is not what happened. We weren't even in a private room; there was no door to close. In fact, Dr. Niro hadn't even pulled our curtain! I was pretty sure that this was bad form; surely if you don't want other people to know your weight, you probably also don't want them to overhear your brand-new diagnosis.

Dr. Niro continued in his blank tone, almost a recitation. "Given your family history with your grandmother, father, and your presenting symptoms, I believe I am able to ascertain your type. You have CMT1A."

"Which of her symptoms make you think it's definitely CMT?" asked my dad.

Dr. Niro turned to my father, and then gestured towards my legs. "She has a drop-foot gait, muscle atrophy in her arms and legs, arched feet, and a tremor, all classic signs."

I jumped in. "A *tremor*?"

Maybe some of those other things were true, but I knew that I definitely didn't shake.

"Hold your hand out and try to keep it still," Dr. Niro said.

This was stupid, but I obeyed the command and held my hand out. I concentrated on keeping it absolutely, perfectly still. Dr. Niro was about to feel very silly for declaring that I had a tremor.

My hand trembled.

I stared at my hand. I had expected to prove the doctor wrong. *Why had no one told me I had a tremor before? Had I been shaking this whole time?*

I didn't understand how my hand was shaking, right in front of me, but I had never noticed it before—not even when my hands were crafting hundreds of tiny little clay cherries and pastries.

I put my arm down and didn't say anything.

"Huh, that's interesting," I heard my dad say to my right. In my peripheral vision I could see him hold his own arm out in front of him.

"You have it too," said Dr. Niro flatly.

It felt like Dr. Niro handed out diagnoses the way people hand out brochures on the street that no one wants or asked for. Except this one we couldn't just throw in the nearest trash can.

My diagnosis turned into prognosis, which wasn't any more romantic or softly delivered than the diagnosis had been.

Dr. Niro started making predictions. He told me that I needed leg braces and that I would likely need surgery on my feet within four years.

This all sounded ridiculous, and I wasn't the only one who thought so.

"My mom didn't need braces until her fifties," my dad said. "And I am only mildly affected. Why do you think she'll progress so rapidly?" He didn't sound concerned, just skeptical.

That's right, Dad, you tell him! I thought.

"There is evidence that CMT gets worse with every generation," said Dr. Niro. "And based on how her symptoms are presenting now... her case is going to be much more severe than you or your mother's."

This was new information that none of us had expected. We were all quiet now. I still didn't really believe Dr. Niro's predictions, but what if they were partly true? What if my CMT was different than my dad's and grandmother's? What did that mean? What would it look like?

Having sufficiently stunned us into silence, Dr. Niro continued: "I'll schedule you for an EMG; it's a nerve conduction study."

"What does that stand for?" I asked.

"Electromyography."

I made a mental note to Google that later. Maybe that would prove more comforting than this.

When the appointment was (finally!) over, we all got in the car and just sat quietly for a minute. Before the silence could fully envelop the car, I made my intentions known.

"I don't like him, and I don't want to get leg braces."

"You don't have to if you don't want to," said my mom. "But right now I have to call May. You know she'll be waiting."

My dad and I nodded. My paternal grandmother, Grandma May, knew that my appointment was today, and that meant she would be waiting by her phone until she got a full report from my mom.

My mom dialed. I listened to her side of the conversation as my dad started driving home.

"It went well."

"He said it definitely looks like CMT."

"Yeah, she's okay."

"They want to do another test. An electro-something?"

"Yeah, that sounds like the one."

"Okay, hold on."

Suddenly she put my grandmother onto speakerphone. "They are NOT doing that test on my baby. Do you hear me, Thomas?"

If Grandma was calling my dad by his full first name, and not "Tom" or "Tommy," I knew she was serious.

"I'm here," he said.

"It's *incredibly* painful." There was sadness in her voice now, as if she was remembering something from long ago that she'd tried hard to forget. "Promise me, Tommy. It doesn't tell them anything new and she doesn't need it."

My dad promised, and he made good. Later that day my mom canceled the appointment.

I was glad that Grandma was looking out for me. I had always been close with my grandmother. My parents and I lived with my grandparents until I was two, and we still would often make the forty-five minute drive to visit them on the weekends. further.

Grandma was pure *grandmother* and everything that that image brings to mind. She kept a huge container shaped like a giant green frog and full of toys in her front room, just in case any children were to stop by. Grandma loved children, all children. But I felt—no, I *knew*—that she loved me most of all.

Grandma would always play games with me, and kept a small collection of board games just for me. My favorite, which we played a lot when I was younger, was Candy Land. I delighted in navigating the Lollipop Woods, visiting the Peanut Brittle House, and hated it when I got stuck in the Molasses Swamp in our race to the Candy Castle. Candy Land was full of surprises. I was very good at Candy Land and won every time against Grandma.

Later, when I was an adult, my father pointed out that the winner of Candy Land is predetermined by the shuffle of the cards. Before the game even begins, destiny is written.

I didn't believe him. It couldn't be random.

"But I won every time," I argued.

He rolled his eyes exaggeratedly to make sure I saw. "Yeah, Grandma cheated so you would win. It's a weird way of cheating, mind you." Grandma had used deception in order to avoid upsetting me.

This was unsettling news; my memories of Candy Land were tarnished lies. What else might she have been keeping from me? What else might not be exactly as I imagined?

While I was playing, I felt like I had control over my character's journey in the game. That I made choices that mattered and influenced the outcome. But that was all imagined. When my cards were dealt, my character's story was decided: come hell or high water, I was headed toward Molasses Swamp. The game was rigged, and I had no way to change it.

Candy Land was just one thing that I saw through different eyes when I was older, and forced to. There are some things you just grow up with, and for you they are normal. Like the fact that grandmas wear leg braces.

We spent a lot of time at Grandma's house, and I would often watch her ritual of taking off her leg braces at night. In a way, it signified the end of the day for me; social hour was done when Grandma's leg braces came off. Everyone else I knew was too young to have braces yet and I liked watching Grandma take them off; it felt intimate and special. It was the only time I saw them, too, since they were otherwise always hidden under Grandma's pant legs. I never saw her in a skirt. Grandma's braces were made of thick, opaque white plastic. They started just below her knees, encompassing most of her legs all the way down to her feet, where they disappeared into her shoes. Grandma wore big white sneaker hybrids, with large velcro straps where the laces should be. The front of the shoes were covered with small holes for ventilation. They weren't very attractive, and I felt bad that Grandma couldn't wear pretty shoes. But then again, grandmas probably didn't care about such things.

As I watched, she would undo the strap at the top of the brace, and then pull off her shoe and brace in one swoop. With shaking hands (which I attributed to age), she would roll down her stocking and take it off. This was usually accompanied by a soft, guttural sigh—one of relief. Bringing her bare foot up to rest on her other knee, she would start to rub it before repeating the process on the other leg. Grandma's feet were small, and often puffy and swollen with marks from her stockings and shoes imprinted in her skin.

When she finished rubbing her feet and the marks had disappeared, she would set her braces, upright and still in her shoes, next to her by the couch. It was a slightly comical sight, like two disembodied legs. They would wait there for her until she needed to get up and go somewhere.

I never saw Grandma walk without them.

2

THOMASINA

"You're so much like your father," my grandmother said. I was seven, and we were standing in her kitchen. She took my round face in her hand, holding my head in place by my chin like she was scolding me. I looked up at her. She was smiling big at me with the corner of her mouth pulled into a slight smirk.

I took her observation as a compliment. I heard it a lot, usually after I said something sarcastic and, in my mind, particularly clever. This time, after my grandmother had asked, "Is broccoli *really* going to hurt you?" I'd said, "It might...."

Letting go of my face, she pushed one of my dark brown curls—so similar to my father's—behind my ear. "Your parents should have named you Thomasina."

I stared down at my bowl of mashed potatoes. They were suspiciously *green*, a color I knew mashed potatoes weren't meant to be. Grandma took her quest to nourish me quite seriously, even if that meant chopping broccoli into almost imperceptible pieces.

Grandma was good at hiding tiny things inside of other things—and at denying their existence if confronted—but I knew, even then, that the tiniest bit of something bad could ruin a thing completely.

The last thing I wanted to do was put this potentially dangerous broccoli in my mouth, but Grandma—whom I loved, and so much, and who had made mashed potatoes just for me—was watching; so I gathered a pile of green mush on my fork and moved it up to my mouth as slowly as I could. I made eye contact with Grandma the entire time, communicating with just my eyes: *Look what you're making me do.* When the fork made it to my mouth and I tasted the green potatoes, I was surprised to discover they were delicious—just like Grandma's mashed potatoes always were. My face gave me away, and Grandma smiled at me with that half smirk again. She knew I'd love it; the recipe had already been tested on the previous generation and several grandchildren before me.

Even if there were hidden bits of something I didn't want, it could still be almost perfect.

Thomasina isn't that bad of a name, I thought.

I liked being compared to my father and wanted to be more like him. I've heard that all little girls idolize their fathers, but my father was different; I *knew* that my father really *was* the smartest and funniest and coolest father I knew. Other girls' fathers I met were usually dull and not interested in playing. They would engage us only when passing by on their way in from work, or to the kitchen, distractedly asking, "You girls having fun?" and continuing on their routes, regardless of the answer. They just asked about homework, or how dance practice had gone, usually with one eye on their computers and another on the newspaper. But my dad was different. He was creative, endlessly involved. He took me, and my friends, on adventures. He was always showing me that the world was something to be questioned and discovered. He took me to all of the museums, fairs, festivals, and any other kid-friendly events in town. But our standard favorite was to walk together, hand in hand, to our nearby park.

Esch Park was small, but it was just two blocks away from our house and featured a clearing with a brightly-colored jungle gym for the local children. The park and jungle gym had all of the staples—slides, monkey bars, swings, a seesaw and even a small sand pit. We used to go every weekend so I could swing and look for squirrels.

The jungle gym was built out of colorful structures, horizontal rods and slats, wooden beams stacked vertically with plastic rocks attached, a sheet of rope weaved together like a web. Some of them went high up to the very top of the play structure.

"What are those for?" I asked my dad after several visits to the park. I pointed to the ladder-like structures.

"Climbing," he said.

Oh. I had thought they were decorative. Climbing? Why would anyone do that... for fun?

"Want to try?" he asked.

"No," I said, without any hesitation.

"Why not?"

"I'll fall." My voice was even. I wasn't scared, I was stating facts.

"Why do you think you'll fall?" he pressed. Dad never let something go.

I looked at the structure in front of us, with its shiny, bright red cylindrical bars. I thought about it; about why my body knew innately that to attempt to grab and climb those bars was a bad idea.

"I can't hold on."

"Interesting," I heard my dad say. I almost didn't hear him; it was as if he was talking more to himself than me. After that he was quiet. We moved on to the swing set, and I was relieved that he didn't push the issue further.

———

There are some things that you instinctively know not to try. Like turning black widow spiders into a bedtime cuddle pet, or seeing if bread mold is delicious. I never once tried to get on one of those structures or swing on the monkey bars, even though I would eventually watch child after child do it with ease. It wasn't lack of interest per se, but a lack of interest that stemmed from a deep wisdom of what I could not do. I knew my hands could not hold their grip on the bars, that no matter how hard I squeezed, my hands would slip off. I knew I would not have the strength to pull my body up. I knew I would not have the footing to get up and back down safely, without falling. My body, I knew—even at age seven—would fail me.

So I made myself content on the swings. The park had a swing set with four identical black swings in a line; from there I could keep a safe distance from the children running around and behaving like monkeys, climbing and hanging upside down while I—more mature, more available for truly great things like swings—swung peacefully with my dad nearby.

Sometimes I would recruit him to push me on the swing, but that brought with it some inherent risks.

"Dad, push *gentle!*" I would always tell him, my words accompanied with a warning glare. The response was usually a very unnerving "Uhuh."

I had reason to be concerned. I preferred a gentle swing, but from time to time he would suddenly tell me to hold on tight. Without giving me time to protest, he would push me *hard*. I would swing high up into the air while he ran underneath me screaming, "UNDER DOG! UNDER DOG!" His screams were joined with my own screams of terror while I held on so tight that my hands turned white. I was always convinced I was going to fall off the swing, but I never did.

"Dad, don't *ever* do that again!" I would always say, after catching my breath and letting my heart rate return to close to normal. But I knew that my father was a force that could not be controlled. Grandma probably had a lot of trouble convincing him to eat green mashed potatoes, too.

Occasionally I went down one of the smaller slides on the climbing structure, but I stayed far away from the large slide. It was bright orange and curled around, taller than three fathers stacked one on top of the other. From the safety of the swing set, I watched other children go down the orange monster of a slide over and over, screaming with excitement the entire time. As soon as they reached the bottom, they would shout, "Again, again!!" and run back up to the top. They could do this for upwards of a dozen times in a row. I was perplexed by this, and assumed that these children were just hyperactive and abnormal.

Once my dad did successfully coax me onto the slide. He had his mind set on it as soon as we'd arrived at the park, on an otherwise lovely summer day. "Hey, Pooh, why don't you go down the slide?" he started.

I ignored the question and continued toward the swings, but the pestering continued.

"Just once."

"Come on, it'll be fun."

"Just try it."

Finally, after several minutes of this, I gave in. I was ready to get it over with so he would stop bugging me and I could swing in peace.

I carefully dismounted from my swing and walked over to the jungle gym that the slide was connected to. Without waiting for me to ask him to, my dad picked me up and set me on the main platform. Now I was on my own. There were a few more steps up to the slide, which I went up slowly—partially to delay the inevitable. But the final step up to the slide was really tall and I didn't know if I could step up it. Instead, I sat down on it and then got on my hands and knees to crawl the rest of the way there—luckily only a couple yards. The hard plastic flooring hurt my hands; when I lifted up my hand to look at it, I could see the floor's woven design already imprinted into my skin. And when I reached the top of the slide, I just sat at the top.

I'd known it was high but I hadn't realized how high it would feel once I got up there. "It's really high!" I called down to my dad, who was standing at the bottom of the slide. I looked over at the swing set. My swing looked so small from here. *Why had I left my swing?*

"It's not really that high," he said.

"It's slippery."

"It's a... slide," he said.

"You're making fun of me!"

"Yes, now go down the slide."

Other kids usually reached the bottom in a couple seconds with a *whoooosh!* But as I inched my body forward, I figured out that I could hug the walls with my palms to ease my descent down the slide. This worked surprisingly well, and instead of a *whooosh*, I made more of a *brp... brpp.... brp...* sound as I slowly went down.

It took close to a minute before I had fully lowered myself to the bottom. I sat at the bottom of the slide, brushing myself off and making a show of dramatically catching my breath.

"What was that?" my dad asked. He was laughing at me.

"I went down the slide," I said. "Are you happy?"

"I guess so…" he said, still laughing. "Want to go down again?"

"No."

He held out his hand to me and we walked back to the swings.

———

Somehow, despite my lack of interest in sports or physical activity of most kinds, I always seemed to have scraped-up knees from falling. Sometimes grownups would ask me, pointing at the bandages on my knees, if I'd been roughhousing. I'd shake my head. "No, I just fall sometimes," I would tell them.

Because that was true. I just fell sometimes.

To avoid tripping all the time I taught myself to look down at my feet while walking. This meant that I was always finding treasures on the ground—buttons, beads, coins—and cool-looking rocks which I brought home in my pockets to add to my collection. Dad bought me a rock tumbler to polish and identify my rocks like a real scientist. He told me about how they had been formed and taught me to look at the world, and everything I touched, like a scientist.

This was ultimately why my dad never made me feel bad about being unathletic: he had other plans for me.

"You're going to be a doctor," my dad told me. The first time I remember him saying that, I was four. But I found out later that he had been telling me this for longer than I'd been forming memories.

I was not so easily persuaded and wasn't yet convinced. "But I want to be a princess!" I declared.

"You can be a princess with a doctorate," he said. Even though he was focussed on my being a medical doctor, he was willing to settle for any sort of PhD.

Even though my aspirations changed over the next few years, from princess to veterinarian and many things in between, his response was always the same.

"You can be a dancer... with a doctorate."

"You can be a singer... with a doctorate."

"You can be a vet... with a doctorate."

I didn't mind. Dad made me feel like I could achieve the highest achievements there were in life. I assumed there was no higher achievement than a doctorate, hence the reason why he chose it for me. He even wrote me my own theme song.

He would sing it to me, arms waving, his voice loud and animated. Whenever Dad was performing, it was a full production.

Bethany, Bethany, Bethany Anne. If she can't do it then nobody can! Becaaaause she's Bethany, Bethany, Bethany, Bethany, Bethany, Bethany Anne!

There was just one problem with the song. Anne wasn't actually my middle name. When I was born, my dad wanted to name me Bethany Anne, and my mom wanted to name me Bethany Noelle. My dad acquiesced and Bethany Noelle is on my birth certificate, but that didn't stop him from pretending that my name was Bethany Anne.

Bethany, Bethany, Bethany Anne.

Slowly, over time, his conditioning worked. Eventually I started saying, "I want to be a doctor when I grow up." And I felt that it was entirely my idea and decision.

My dad showed me that if you are committed to pretending something is true, in time others will start to believe it too. That if you do a good enough job of just keeping the fiction alive, even *you* will forget that it wasn't true in the first place.

―――――

Part of my dad's project of grooming me to become a scientist was teaching me to have a sense of scientific skepticism. When I was four, my dad was driving my grandfather's van and I was in the front seat looking out the window.

Suddenly, my window went down. I was startled. In our car you had to roll down your window by cranking the hand lever. I knew windows didn't just move by themselves.

"What was that?" I said. "Dad! ... did you do that?"

"What?" he said. "Maybe it was a ghost."

I was not yet attuned to my father's sarcasm or tendency to make things up to mess with me or teach me a lesson, so I took him at face value and was convinced there was a ghost in the van who chose to haunt us... by letting in a gentle breeze.

It stopped, and I relaxed. I felt comfortable that the danger had passed.

Suddenly my window started moving up and down again on its own.

"DADDY!" I said, jumping back from the window and sinking low into my seat for protection.

"Is *this* your ghost?" he said. He pointed to the automatic window opener on his side of the car. He was pushing it up and down.

"You tricked me!" I frowned, scrunching up my whole face so he could see how epically annoyed I was.

"Yes," he said. "And I'm also teaching you something: don't assume that something you don't understand is a ghost." He looked disappointed in me. I didn't want to disappoint him again and resolved to be smarter—and not afraid of ghosts.

Not long after, my mom's brother called her and told her that his family's house was being haunted. He described the poltergeist's effects: knick-knacks being moved; unexplained whiffs of perfume; water bottles flying off the table; doors shaking violently. He further explained that they had learned a Native American burial ground had been dug up nearby. That had to be the cause of the haunting.

My mom repeated her brother's story to my dad and me, in full, ghostly detail. At the end, I was feeling sick with fear—we were going to be visiting them and sleeping over at their house in a couple months!

My dad wasn't impressed by the story. "Oh yes, air currents," he said. "Very frightening."

This brought me out of my fear and reminded me of the lesson Dad had taught me.

"Yeah," I said to my mom. "You shouldn't assume something you don't understand is a ghost."

I looked over to my dad. He was smiling; I could tell he was proud.

———

Besides, I had much more terrifying things to worry about than the possibility of ghosts. At Sunday School, which I attended... religiously... I was occasionally forced to participate in a sick ritual. Stay with me here.

The ritual involved sitting in a circle with other children. One of us was chosen to walk around the circle to select her victim. She stood behind us, one by one, tapping each of us on the head to establish her authority and incite fear.

On those dark days when this ritual was enacted, I was forced to sit in the circle, unable to stop what was about to happen, completely paralyzed by fear.

As the Chosen One walked around the circle, I prayed silently to myself. *Please not me, please not me, please not me...*

I closed my eyes when I could hear her getting closer.

Please not me, please not me, I continued to pray as I could hear the Chosen One approach...

...until she was behind me, and tapped me on the head, shouting "Duck!"

My body collapsed in relief. This meant I had not been chosen.

But someone still needed to be, and a few seconds later I heard "GOOSE!"

I watched as one child chased the other; I felt bad for the goose, being forced to jump up so quickly and run after the other. If he didn't catch her in time, then he would have to choose the next victim, and be chased.

But as I watched, I noticed something completely, totally weird. I was taught to be a rational scientist, but this was something I couldn't explain.

They seemed to be having fun.

3

ARE YOU HAPPY?

Sometimes I wished I could get sick. It seemed so glamorous. I imagined that if I were sick I'd be allowed to eat as many popsicles and fudgesicles from the freezer as I wanted. Dad would make me noodles with butter and salt for dinner, and Mom would surround me with fluffy pillows on the couch while I watched *The Parent Trap II* over and over again. I would be my parents' first priority at all times, and they would be glad to stop whatever less important things they were doing to meet my every whim—no matter how over the top. (*I wanted orange popsicles, not cherry. This fluffy pillow is not fluffy enough. This pillow is too fluffy.*)

I didn't have to wish for long. I had been homeschooled for the previous two years, but in my first month of third grade, the cesspool of germs that is a children's classroom granted me my first infection—although I didn't get sick the way my classmates did before me.

They had colds. Sniffles. Maybe the flu if we're getting creative. But me? When I got sick, I got *Streptococcus*, a.k.a. strep throat. On the day my mom took me to see my pediatrician, Dr. Dayton, he held my tongue down with a large popsicle stick.

"Say ahhHHHHH," he said, his large greying mustache

bouncing as he spoke. It (the mustache) made it impossible for anything he said to come across as threatening; sometimes I would imagine that his mustache was a small animal perched on his lip with only its tufts of grey fur visible.

As soon as I said "ahhHHH," it felt like he tried to jab the stick down my throat. I started gagging as he removed it. He looked satisfied and walked out of the room with his sample. Despite his choking me with a popsicle stick, I liked Dr. Dayton. He spoke to me kindly, not as if I were a small, stupid child the way some grownups did. His touch was soft. He always smiled when I saw him, and the many lines around the outside corners of his eyes suggested that he was someone who smiled even when he didn't have to.

Strep results come back fast; within three minutes the mustache—and its owner—returned.

"Yep, she has strep," he said to my mom. This time he spoke to her, not me.

I hadn't heard of strep before, but it sounded like something bad. That must make it even more glamorous. Surely, strep was way cooler than the common cold, which even had "common" in its name.

I hadn't imagined my throat would feel so raw and sore while I was sick, but aside from that, all of my dreams came true. I was right: being sick meant unlimited popsicles, big bowls of buttery noodles, and being allowed to do nothing but just watch movies. I was pampered. I was special. I had everything I wanted.

When I was well enough to return to school a few days later, the enjoyment of my illness continued. My teachers and classmates all asked what was wrong and told me how sorry they felt for me. I told them about strep and they seemed impressed. I was right again; it was way more glamorous than a cold.

Our Montessori classroom didn't assign homework, and so I wasn't assigned a stack of papers to catch up on. The lessons I had missed, my teachers took the time to teach me one-on-one. Miss Boffi and I lay on the carpeted classroom floor as she taught me how to do long division.

"Divide Multiply Subtract Bring down... just remember Dad Mom Sister Brother," she explained.

"Dad Mom Sister Brother," I repeated.

I liked having my teachers' full attention. I felt special and lucky to have extra attention that my classmates weren't getting. This was a benefit of being sick that I hadn't expected, and I couldn't wait to discover what other unexpected gifts my brief foray into illness would bring me.

Less than a week later, my second infection was granted. This time it was an ear infection, and while it was more exciting, it also hurt worse than the strep had; I was no longer as enthused about only having the energy to sit in front of the TV. Even the popsicles had started to lose their previous appeal.

But the ear infection introduced me to the magical elixir that is liquid Amoxicillin.

When we filled my prescription, we received a little bottle full of a bright pink goop accompanied by a plastic dosing spoon. I thought that a medicine disguised by such a pretty color must be hiding an even nastier flavor than usual.

I was wrong. It was bubblegum-flavored—insanely delicious. I had found the upside of ear infections and whenever I was taking Amoxicillin, I would ask, "Mom, can I have the medicine yet?" the way children ask *Are we there yet?* during long car rides.

After the strep and ear infections, I felt like I had successfully *done* illness. I had seen the other side, eaten close to forty popsicles and fudgesicles in a three-week period, and watched *The Parent Trap II* five times. I now knew that you could find God inside the bright pink liquid of the little bottle in our fridge.

But I had missed school. I adored my teachers, Miss Boffi and Ms. Fritz, whose names reminded me of fantasy characters from the Roald Dahl books my dad read to me. They were kind and funny and I knew that they loved me, in the same admiring way that I loved them. At recess I would walk with them and talk to them the whole time, while my classmates played soccer and swung from monkey bars.

My Montessori school, as is typical for the style, had a self-paced philosophy and, aside from group lessons, we worked alone and could choose what to work on. During group lessons I was dedicated to being the best to get the love and approval of my teachers. But the rest of the time, without a teacher watching me, I was unmotivated to work; I carefully figured out a system of how to look busy and keep my assignment chart full without ever doing anything very hard.

When I did learn, I enjoyed it. Miss Boffi taught us how to tell time; Ms. Fritz taught us how to write in cursive. One time in class while I was admiring my loopy letters, Frances—who was popular—looked at my paper and told me I had the prettiest cursive writing in class.

I was ready to put my illness experiences behind me and move on with being a pretty cursive writer and a tricky student. But that's not what happened. What I learned, instead, was that when wishes come true, it isn't always the way you had wanted them to. And that it's often too late to change the terms.

Rather than subsiding, the mysterious infections kept coming. It seemed that as each one left, it made room for the next one to take up residence in my body. The final count was five ear infections and three throat infections within the first few months of third grade. I wondered why I had ever wished for this in the first place; illness wasn't popsicles and noodles, it was pain and isolation. It meant no recess, no show-and-tell, no time looking into the class microscope.

When the infections did finally stop coming—finally defeated after an onslaught of antibiotics—they left room for something new to take their place: severe and near-constant stomach pains.

I had become a frequent visitor of Dr. Dayton's, so when my mom and I walked in for an appointment to address the stomach pains, he was ready to write me another prescription for antibiotics. My mom stopped him. "It's something new this time," she said. "This is different."

I showed him where it hurt, told him how it felt like stabbing and throbbing at the same time, and that it kept happening, sometimes for hours. He told me he would need to put his hand underneath my dress—I always wore dresses; I loved how they made me feel pretty and princessy—to feel my belly.

He lifted up my dress and pressed his hand where I told him it hurt. Even though his touch was still gentle, his hand felt hard and cold. Having someone touch my stomach felt so much more intimate than a popsicle stick on my tongue or a flashlight in my ear. His fingers pressed deeper into my stomach, searching for clues. He searched not only my stomach, but my eyes—which he would look down into every time he pressed in a new spot. What was he looking for? A wince? Probably, I thought. But the pain remained constant and didn't care about his touch, which made it neither better or worse. I just sat, watching him—meeting his eyes when they searched mine—hoping for the pain to reveal itself to him so that the examination could be over.

He had bent down to be closer to my level, and when he rose there was no immediate declaration of diagnosis as we were used to.

I fixed my dress, flattening out all of its wrinkles against my legs; I made a mental note to remember not to wear a dress next time, if there was a next time.

I was learning that there would always be a next time.

We left without an answer and without any bubblegum flavored medicine to make it all better. We were recommended to hope that "the pain will eventually go away on its own." These things tended to clear up by themselves.

Instead, the pain got worse. I was missing even more school than I had from the infections; sometimes my mom would find me crying on the kitchen floor when we needed to leave for school. "I can't go," I would tell her, tears streaming down my cheeks. Sometimes she would hold me right there on the floor, pulling me close to her chest, where she would rock me like an infant. Our kitchen flooring was hard, cold white tile—not the most comfortable to lie on, but neither of us noticed. Mom was always the person I ran to when I was hurting, and right now the only person who I felt could understand.

"I'm so sorry, Bethany," she would tell me, wiping the tears from my face with her hand. "I wish I knew what to do." Her voice was shaky, and I knew not to look at her face—couldn't bear to see her own tears—or how her mouth would open, as if she was about to speak, but no words came out—searching for the right thing to say, for anything that could make it better.

She would always manage to say that it would all be okay, that all of this was just temporary—and I knew that she was speaking to both of us.

Other times she seemed frustrated with me and forced me to go despite my tears.

"Do you just not want to go, or can you really *not* go?" she would ask me. I hated when she asked me that, and for a brief moment, I thought I hated her. Hated her for the doubting of my truth that I felt come through in her question—for making me feel even more isolated in the inherent loneliness and despair of unrelenting pain.

Sometimes she asked the question out of frustration, but that was almost better than when her tone was one of pure desperation, when I could hear her hope that I was just exaggerating. I almost always did go to school then, out of guilt for making her feel that way. *She's right*, I thought, *I can go if I really try.*

But when I did make it to school, I often wouldn't make it through the day before the pain got so bad that my mom had to come and get me. When Miss Boffi or Ms. Fritz saw me come up to them, they knew it was probably to ask to use the phone.

Since I didn't need my tongue depressed or another dose of bubblegum medicine, Dr. Dayton soon ran out of ideas and things he could do to fix me.

We went to more doctors—gastroenterologists, chronic disease specialists, allergists—who all put their cold hands on my stomach and wanted several vials of my blood for tests. I soon became an expert at being pricked by needles. When the nurse picked up my right arm to draw blood (eight times out of ten), I would confidently tell her, "You want the other arm. The left is my good arm."

The nurse would then examine my left arm and inevitably coo over how big and pretty the vein on it was. I loved being so knowledgeable, even as I hated the subject.

I always watched the needles go in when they drew my blood. The nurses would warn me to look away, but I would just keep staring at the blue vein on my arm, watching the needle slide in. I wanted to know exactly what was being done to me and when, to know that I was still the one in control of my body.

It turns out, those were the easy tests.

One of the doctors ordered an upper endoscopy.

"We will put you to sleep," the nurse explained. "And then we'll send a little camera down your throat to take pictures." She was the first person to explain the procedure to me, just ten minutes before it was going to happen.

I imagined the little camera on its journey down my esophagus and intestines. I hoped it would be safe and would find out what was wrong inside me.

"Can I take the pictures home?" I asked.

The nurse gave me a look like I had asked a weird or wrong question, but confirmed that, yes, I could have a copy of the pictures.

When the nurse left, a doctor I didn't know came up to my hospital bed. "I'm Dr. Bird," he said. "Are you ready to take a quick nap?"

"Yes," I said. "Can I have the pictures after?" I reasoned that the more people I asked, the greater the chance of me actually getting the pictures.

I don't remember what Dr. Bird's response was—or if he even replied at all—because, just like that, I woke up.

I wouldn't have known that the procedure had already happened, or that anything had happened at all, were it not for the wave of nausea that hit me as soon as I opened my eyes.

I started heaving and a shallow blue bucket appeared on my lap, held by a nurse who had waited in anticipation for this moment. I bent over the bucket and vomited violently, until my whole body felt weak. For a brief moment I felt that intense relief after you vomit out sickness, but it didn't last, and a moment later I felt the next wave of nausea roll through me. I clutched the sides of the bucket with sweaty palms, riding through each wave and knowing that I had no control over them. I vomited four times, one after another in quick succession, until I had nothing left to give—I was only vomiting up stomach acid and saliva.

Staring at my bucket full of sickly yellow vomit, I wondered how I could ever have thought that illness was glamorous.

The little camera hadn't found out what was wrong, but I proudly took its pictures of my insides to show-and-tell the next day. I marveled at the photos: the smooth sliminess of my esophagus, delicate pink folds of the inside of my stomach, and the wrinkles of my intestines—like they were wearing a sweater that was too big for them. This was so much cooler than looking at the slides in our classroom microscope, this was my *body* in a way I had never seen or known it before.

I stared at those photos and wondered if I looked at them hard enough, maybe I could see what the doctor couldn't—see what the answer to my pain was. If only I knew what to look for.

Shortly after the endoscopy, I had another test—an upper GI visualization.

When I walked into yet another cold room (the rooms were always freezing, for reasons I could never figure out), the tech explained that I was going to drink a radioactive fluid and they would watch it go through my gastrointestinal system on an x-ray and look for problems.

"You need to drink this," he said, handing me a tall glass. "And keep drinking it. Don't stop."

I looked down at the glass. It was full of frothy white liquid; small bubbles came up to the surface. There was a straw in it.

I took a tentative sip.

I had chosen to be here. The doctor who ordered this test had given us two choices: upper GI or lower GI test. He didn't explain the difference or the benefits of one over the other; they seemed to be interchangeable. As my mom drove me home from the consult, she told me I could pick.

My mom let me make a lot of choices. What to eat for dinner, what to wear, whether I wanted to go to school.

I knew that these were the most important choices though— of what was going to be done to my body next—and appreciated that she knew they belonged to me.

Mom told me that in the lower GI test they would send a camera up my butt. I was surprised by how frank she was being, so I knew that she must have really wanted to get across the potential gravity of the internal photo shoot. I didn't know what the upper GI involved and she didn't seem to either, but we both felt sure that it was the better option. It didn't involve the butt.

But now I wondered if there had been a choice at all. If this didn't work, they would want to do a lower GI—wouldn't they? If there was a choice, why was it mine? Shouldn't there have been an obvious answer, a course of action given to us by my doctor?

Did they not know either?

Were all of these tests just so we would have something to

do, to feel like we were doing something in the search of getting better?

The room was cold. Not just cold in temperature, but so barren and icy that it made you feel cold when you looked at it; grey walls met grey floors in a room with only two large metal examination beds and complicated-looking equipment. I didn't know what the equipment did, except even the machines were grey and looming and even they made me feel cold.

My mom was in the room but I couldn't see her now, couldn't feel her warmth. It was just me and this tall glass of an unknown liquid, and my desire to believe that it would lead us to an answer.

I took a sip, and I was surprised to discover that radioactive fluids were cherry-flavored. It actually tasted kind of good, like a cherry slushy but thicker.

I kept drinking as the tech moved me into a reclined position and pointed to a nearby screen. I could see the skeleton of my torso and a white mass of liquid moving down my GI tract.

Cool, I thought. *This test isn't even hard, it's kind of fun.*

As I kept drinking, the cherry-flavored fluid seemed to get thicker, chalky. What started as something fun and intriguing was quickly turning into something vile. I started to sweat; my body wanted me to stop drinking and to get rid of this poison.

But I had to keep drinking, couldn't stop drinking. Not because to stop would be "bad"—although it would be disobedient—but because I needed to believe that I was doing this for a reason, that there was a reason for all of it. Maybe if I suffered enough now, I wouldn't have to suffer from stomach pains.

The room was still cold, but my body was hot, and at the end of the test I couldn't leave the room—I believed that if I moved I would vomit. My mom came over and held me while I cried and we waited for the nausea to pass. This time it wasn't like the quick crashing waves after the endoscopy, but a constant heaviness that enveloped me, overtook me. My body was moving, spinning—or was it the room?—but I couldn't open my eyes now to look, looking only made it worse.

The upper GI test came back negative.

Because the tests always came back negative.

At night I would wonder if this was all my fault. *Is this what I get for asking to be sick in the first place?* I would have done anything to take it all back.

Some of the doctors waited until after their tests came back negative to start asking The Questions. Others just jumped right in on the first visit.

"Do you like school?"

"Do you have friends?"

"Is anyone mean to you?"

…

"Are you happy?"

———

My mom, desperate to fix her daughter, prepared me various drinks every morning, made of powders mixed with water or extracts from plants that the packages claimed contained healing properties. The labels all read versions of: "Immune-boosting" - "antibacterial" - "antioxidants" - "super food" - "energy boosting" - "cancer prevention."

Each time she brought one home she showed it to me and rattled off all of its touted benefits. "A friend said it cured her friend's cousin's irritable bowel," she'd say one day. The next time she may have been recommended an herbal tincture by a very convincing and nice lady at Whole Foods, who happened to be selling the product.

Regardless of who told her about them, they all tasted wretched. I argued with her about why "cancer healing" wasn't relevant to me (I didn't have cancer, I had stomach pain and fatigue), but she would just tell me I still needed to drink it anyway.

Even though I could see her face light up with hope every time she handed me a new concoction, they didn't make *me* feel better. They made me feel nauseated and bitter that I had to drink horrible mud just to make my mom feel better; I was the one who was suffering. She stopped pushing most of the drinks and powders after a couple of weeks, but she continued preparing one of the "immune-boosting" vitamin shakes every morning. It was an unsettling beige color and had a viscous, gritty texture. I gagged while drinking it, and the process could take up to an hour before I got it all down.

After a few months of this, I started sneaking to the downstairs bathroom and pouring it down the sink. I couldn't stand the taste one more time, but I also didn't want my mom to lose the single thread of hope that there was still a chance I could get better.

We escalated. We tried Vitamin C and magnesium cocktails through IV's that I watched drip into my (good) arm; weekly shots of B12 (which had to go right into my butt); oils that made me have accidents in the middle of class; cutting out sugar and dairy from my diet; acupuncture; pain patches; prayer; and more tests.

Eventually, negative results for even horrible diseases and illnesses were disheartening.

Negative for mono.

Negative for lupus.

Negative for Lyme.

At this point I would have taken a positive, even if it was bad news. All we wanted were answers.

We continued to see Dr. Dayton occasionally, both out of loyalty to him for being my original doctor, and because we knew and trusted him. He continued to run the same blood tests that the other doctors had.

One year after the pains began, we sat in his office waiting for him to arrive. I was perched on the exam table, my legs dangling off and swinging slowly. The pain was especially bad today.

I was staring at the room's wallpaper border, which pictured cartoon children meant to represent children from around the world. Each one looked completely different from the last, except for two features: they all had comically large cartoon-style heads, and all of them were smiling. One had orange hair and freckles with brown cowboy boots and a matching hat, another wore a grass skirt with a purple flower lei around her neck and had cute little bare feet.

My mom saw me staring at the wall.

"What are you thinking?" she asked.

"I am counting how many of the children have shoes, to distract myself from the pain," I said, still staring at the wall.

My mom was quiet, and when I looked over at her, her face looked anguished and her eyes were full of tears.

At the end of the appointment, Dr. Dayton asked to speak with my mom alone in the hall.

I didn't know what Dr. Dayton told my mom, but I knew it made her angry because she slammed the car door and the front door when we got home, too. You could always tell when my mom was angry, even if she didn't say so.

Later she told me that Dr. Dayton told her she should take me to a psychologist, and confirmed what I'd suspected: that that was why the other doctors asked those irrelevant Questions, and that many of them told her the same thing privately, too.

I no longer wore dresses; I had stopped after what felt like the twentieth doctor I visited had just put his hand up my dress with no warning. My life involved so many strangers touching and examining my body that I wanted to limit their access so that at least I'd have that tiny moment of control. At school during lunch I would always grab my pink lunchbox and go sit at a single desk to eat alone. Sickness wasn't an exciting story anymore (*"strep! oooooh"*); instead it made me feel different in a bad way, as if I were no longer able to access the innocent world and dynamics of the classroom. I missed so much school and was living such a different childhood than my classmates were, and it was easier—felt safer—to avoid them than to risk rejection.

One day I came up to Miss Boffi to ask to use the classroom phone again.

"I'm sorry," I said. "My stomach really hurts. Can I call my mom?"

"It's okay," she said. "You don't have to ask anymore. Just go ahead and use it when you need to."

———

The tests and ideas only got more eccentric as the doctors, and we, got more desperate.

One practitioner had me hold vials of potential allergens in my outstretched arms while he pressed seemingly random spots on my body and then left the room for thirty minutes while I listened to rhythmic drumming music.

I was skeptical of this guy and his method from the start. We had been referred to him by a friend of my mom's, but even my mom admitted that "it does sound a little bizarre." At this point though, we were willing to try almost anything, at least once.

When he returned to the room, my arms were painfully tired and sore and I now hated the sound of the drum. After several weeks of this, with only perpetually sore arms to show for it, I told my mom I didn't want to see him again—that it was a waste of time and money—and we stopped going.

Another one touched my head while grunting; another promised me spiritual-psychic healing; still another told me I had to unearth my deepest demons; another said that if I just pressed a little spot between my thumb and index finger I'd reset my vagus nerve.

Another doctor suggested I keep a dream journal; I was ten now, and seriously doubted that the answers to the pain I had been experiencing for the last three years were hidden in my dreams. I had no intention of writing down my dreams for some stranger, and was irritated that after an hour-long exam and appointment—and even three years in, each appointment gave me a shred of hope that maybe this would be the one—he could offer me nothing.

As each doctor seemed to give up on me, I gave up on them being able to help me, and gave up on my body ever getting better. Maybe this was as good as my body was going to get.

When asked how I was, I'd just say: "I'm fine."

4

THE OLD WOMAN

The hill was small—I know that in retrospect and did then, too—but the slight incline made walking an even more exhausting process than it already was. I was fourteen now, and was headed to The Power Center for the Performing Arts, a playhouse in Ann Arbor, where my freshman class was going to see *Julius Caesar*.

Walking had gotten harder since I had been diagnosed with Charcot-Marie-Tooth disease a year and a half before. It wasn't a slow decline, but it *was* subtle—a gradual worsening every day that I didn't even recognize was happening until I found myself thinking *Wait, I don't remember this hill being so hard to walk up before. Actually, I don't even remember a hill being here at all.*

(It was a small hill, not really a hill at all.)

And when I looked around at my gaggle of classmates, they didn't seem to realize we were going up a hill either. Their movements looked effortless, while I felt like I was trudging through mud with each step. The kind of mud that sticks to you in thick glops, pulling you back down with it, refusing to let you go. The kind of mud that, when you finally get a leg out of its grasp, the freedom is a brief moment before you have to set that leg back down in the mud again. And repeat. But just as that invisible mud refused to let me walk with ease, I refused to fall too far behind—to single myself out from the group, or to let them see that something was wrong. My classmates wouldn't know. *Couldn't* know.

I could see the Power Center now. It wasn't an immediately impressive building, not the kind you stop to look at. A perfect rectangle, it had a flat concrete roof—light grey—and wide concrete columns along its exterior. The concrete gave it a subdued appearance and an unpretentious quality, but its true beauty was in the floor-to-ceiling windows that lined the front of the building.

I saw her then, in the grand windows of the Power Center. She was old, probably at least in her seventies or eighties, judging by the frailty I could recognize even in her flickering reflection.

(Is it impolite to stare at someone, if she can't see you?)

A small, evil part of me was glad to see that someone else recognized we were going up a hill, and that there was someone struggling much more than I was—and *much* more visibly. This was only a small consolation, given that she was about eighty, but it was a consolation nonetheless.

My eyes stayed mostly cast down toward my feet, making sure I didn't trip, but whenever I could, I grabbed a quick stolen glance at her, my new companion, in my peripheral vision. She was hunched over and, in the glass, I could see her struggle as she made her way up the hill. More than just seeing, I could feel her struggle as I watched her take her slow, calculated, small steps. She had probably been strong once, tall—with effortless steps—but time and age had taken their toll, as they always do.

She was heading up to the Power Center too, and as my classmates and I got closer to those expansive glass windows, her reflection grew, too, and became clear.

Suddenly, I found myself face to face with her.

She looked back at me, confused. Blinked twice.

There had never been an old woman. I had been looking at my own reflection the whole time.

5

TINY MISTAKES

Rule #1 For Surviving School: Avoid stairs a.k.a. Public Enemy #1. I have always—since I could walk—gone up stairs with my right leg leading. This fact alone means that it already takes me about twice as long to ascend a staircase—let alone having a degenerative nerve disease. Add high schoolers trying to rush up the stairs behind me? No, thanks.

Every time I thought about walking upstairs, I pictured how mortified I'd feel if my classmates got stuck behind me on a staircase—how annoyed they would be that I was so slow, and then, inevitably, the questions I imagined would be whispered just as soon as the speaker thought I was out of earshot:

What is wrong with her?
I heard it was something with an accident?
Do you think she was born like this?
Ugh honestly I'm so grateful that isn't me
I feel so guilty saying this but like—can you imagine?
We should be nicer to her
I know but—
Ugh I feel super guilty now
Better her than me though, you know? Honestly?

In public buildings where I had to get to the second or third or fifteenth floor, I could usually sneak away from the group and take an elevator. But if stairs were unavoidable, I always went up last, or just waited—pretending to be deeply interested in a window frame or a speck of dirt on the wall—until no one who could pass judgment on me was left.

It wasn't just that I was physically slow at going up stairs. Over the two years since my diagnosis, I had lost the strength to go up even one step without holding on to either a hand railing or a parental arm. (I didn't let anyone else help me.) I discovered this development shortly after my diagnosis, when I went trick-or-treating for the last time.

We discovered that night—me dressed as a hippie, my father dressed as a ghoul—that I could no longer go up the couple of steps to our neighbors' porches without my father's help, something that hadn't been a problem just the year before. Even he seemed surprised by my sudden decline. It was easy to pass off that I was too old to trick-or-treat, but really I stopped because of how hard it was, and the shame of our neighbors seeing me struggle was too much for me to bear.

The abrupt ending to my trick-or-treating career was one thing, but what if I were invited to a party at a classmate's house and I couldn't get up the steps to her front door? I imagined all of my horrifying options in that situation. I could yell for help—"Help! I can't get up your front step!"; on reflection, no, definitely not. I could crawl, but then I'd have to figure out how to stand back up, and I'd be left with bruised knees on top of a bruised ego. I could sit out there alone on that front step until my mom came to pick me up. Or, I could have her help me up the couple of steps and then convince her to scatter before ringing the doorbell. But what if there were more steps inside?

It was much easier and safer to just avoid any potential danger altogether, and turn down most invitations.

There was one party I really wanted to attend; it was an all-ages party at a classmate's house that my parents were also invited to. Her family was beyond wealthy, which I knew meant that their house would be very large, which I knew also meant there would be a lot of stairs.

I begged off, of course: "I'm too tired tonight, you guys go without me." And so my parents went, and when they got home my mom couldn't wait to tell me about how she'd excused my absence to the hostess—my classmate's mother—by telling her, "Bethany doesn't do so great with stairs."

The response? "Oh, she could have come! We have an elevator!"

———

It was clear well before my diagnosis that I was not going to excel athletically, but I was taught that that was okay as long as I excelled academically. Intelligence was the most valued quality in the extended Meloche family, the one thing that was praised and fostered above all else.

This was a relief, since as a child I was told that I was smart by lots of people, although I wondered how they knew that, and secretly suspected that people are more likely to think you're smart if you are quiet and don't talk much (which was the case for me). Along with telling me I was smart, people I didn't know would start conversations declaring that they could tell how quiet and shy I was, as if that has ever made a truly shy person want to suddenly open up.

My father told me I was smart, too—or at least "above average"—and when he said it, I believed it. To me he was the clear expert. He was very smart and, although he lightly praised me, he always made sure to let me know that while there were some signs that I had above-average intelligence (although occasionally he had doubts), I was not as smart as he was... and should never be so deluded as to think so.

I *was* expected to be a doctor, or a Doctor (of Philosophy), or to do something smart and equally well-paying, and my life's trajectory—which would include college, a good one—was non-negotiable.

This meant that I needed to get good grades, and to practice not just being smart, but learning how to put that down on paper and for it to be recognized. To be born smart was helpful, but it was not enough; success meant hard work. To craft a perfect balance in my psyche—one where I believed I could achieve excellence, but that resting on my God-given (or genetics-given) intellect would not be enough—required a continual building up and building down of my self-esteem by my father.

"What do we call second place?" my dad asked me almost weekly, imitating a drill sergeant.

"First loser!" I responded, as I had been coached to since I could talk.

My father tells me today that I am his most successful experiment in operant conditioning, and whether you approve of the method or not, you can't deny that the conditioning worked to some extent. I anxiously awaited every test score and wasn't afraid to argue each one to a higher grade.

"A grade earned through arguing is worth more than if you'd earned it in the first place," my dad told me, more than once, when I was in high school.

When I got half credit on a Geology exam question, I did my own research and delivered seven pages of sources that corroborated my argument for full credit to my teacher at his desk. He upped my grade, but I'm also pretty sure he started avoiding me in the halls.

In other words, I was a delight to teach.

And so, when I approached my Art History teacher, Ms. Amrine, and inquired about a test we had taken earlier that week and when we'd get our grades back, she could probably sense my anxiety. She very kindly told me that she would call me, personally, at home that night after she'd finished grading our papers.

Sure enough, that night my mom came in my room holding the home phone. "Ms. Amrine is on the phone for you," she said, handing me the receiver.

"Hello?" I said.

"Hello, Bethany!" Ms. Amrine always sounded cheerful. "I have your test score for you."

"Oh?"

"You got a 99%!"

"Oh, good, thanks." I felt as enthusiastic as if I'd just heard I had a dentist appointment the next day.

I could tell by the rest of our short conversation that my response had disappointed her—of course it had—as she was excited to deliver what she thought was amazing news. And she was probably equally confused by my lack of joy.

I told my dad the score the next day.

"That's great," he replied genuinely, and then, after only the barest pause to let the approval sink in, added, "but why not 100%?"

My 99% should have been—*was*—good enough. But sometimes one error, one small mistake, can cause the whole system to crumble.

I could get a perfect score if I tried hard enough or argued my case well enough. Ultimately, I could control my test scores, but what I couldn't fix—and what I would have given anything to be able to fix—was the single, actually *tiny* mistake in my genetic code that gave me CMT type 1A.

It really was a very small mistake, too. A single mutation of a gene on chromosome 17. This gene, called PMP22, carries instructions for producing peripheral myelin protein 22—a small component of myelin. Myelin is the fatty white substance that coats and insulates our peripheral nerves, similar to how a wire is surrounded by plastic insulation.

It was a small mistake that gave me an extra copy of PMP22— three copies instead of two—that proves, once and for all, that you *can* have too much of a good thing. That extra copy leads to abnormal, patchy myelin, and ultimately nerve damage and nerve death.

These were the facts that I read late at night online—trying to understand the workings of my body, to see what it had in store for me—and wishing that my genes hadn't gotten that *one* question wrong.

Of course, to add insult to injury, Charcot-Marie-Tooth is a *terrible* name.

Named for the three physicians who first described it in 1886 (two French, one English—Tooth), I, like most diagnosed with CMT, wished that Dr. Howard Tooth had stayed out of the whole thing—or at least had a less unfortunate name to lend to our disease.

My diagnosis *didn't* explain the stomach pains that had plagued me as a child, although thankfully they had died down over the years and now an attack was rare. I was much more concerned with how I was going to keep things together when my nerves were unraveling a little more each day.

And even though I worked hard to hide my CMT and believed I was successful, as soon as it sensed I was getting cocky—that I felt I finally had control over it—it quickly knocked me off my feet.

Literally. It made me fall.

I was falling every few months now, and didn't believe my dad when he told me that some people can go a whole decade—or more!—without falling. I assumed that everyone fell periodically, and sometimes fell for no apparent reason at all.

When you fall frequently, you get to practice the art of the fall. A great fall is not only graceful—or as graceful as a fall can be—but is one that causes the minimum amount of damage and injury.

I was able to put in practice all that I had learned the first time I fell at school.

I was walking down the hallway to get something out of my locker, when I tripped (over nothing) and felt myself begin to fall. Tucking my legs in I fell down slowly—and yes, artfully—into a cross-legged seated position.

I decided to act as though I had just decided to sit cross-legged in front of the lockers in the middle of the hallway. Grabbing my backpack, I pretended that I was looking for something in it—something very important that I needed to see up close, from a ground-level vantage point.

Looking up from my clever cover-up, I got the eye of my Geology professor, the one I thought was avoiding me, who was staring at me from across the hall. With a raised eyebrow, he gave me a look that said, *I know what you're up to.*

I looked away.

———

There are few things worse for an academic overachiever than showing up for an exam woefully underprepared.

Such was the case for Anatomy & Physiology, my freshman year. We had been given a study guide, or practice test, the day before our exam, which was several pages long and which I didn't do. Well, I did about 20% of it.

I was tired.

I had a headache.

I didn't feel like it!

But are any of these valid excuses when they are true more often than not? When maybe I should have just gotten used to them?

Laziness is also a very bad quality for an academic over-achiever. That was how I felt when, with my incomplete practice test in my bag, our enthusiastic teacher Ms. Sprout announced that the practice test *was* our test—it was identical. "Surprise! Good news! Good luck!" Yes, very good news, and a ton of luck, *if* you'd done the practice test.

I began to panic—that heart racing, suddenly-the-room-feels-like-100 degrees and you're in a hot sweat kind of panic. I knew how hard this test was and felt certain that I was going to fail—badly.

We passed around the stack of tests, and taking mine, I saw the opportunity.

When I knew that no one was watching, I slipped it into my bag and pulled out the practice test.

We started taking the test, mine already 20% completed. I knew I was cheating, but I told myself all of the lies we tell ourselves when we want to do something shitty. That someone else would have done the same. That it wasn't really cheating because I hadn't practiced the other 80% anyway. That, come to think of it, didn't I kind of deserve a break, just once?

Before we began, Ms. Sprout told us that any other facts we'd learned in the class that didn't show up on the test could be written on the back for half an extra credit point each. I filled up the entire back page of the test with every anatomy and physiology fact I could think of—the words getting tinier and tinier toward the bottom, the writing getting more frantic by the line.

And then I turned my test in and prayed.

I was nervous walking up to Ms. Sprout's desk later that week to collect my test—unsure if I'd passed.

When I reached the front of the line, she looked up at me and exclaimed, "You got the highest grade in class!"

For a brief moment, I was delighted. Then I remembered. The guilt only intensified when she handed me my test.

I had scored 127%.

"Highest grade!!" was scrawled out in red ink and underlined—twice. Two big smiley faces were drawn next to it.

————

Two years after my diagnosis, I met with a different neurologist, Dr. Green, after asking my parents never to send me back to Dr. Niro again. (I could never forgive him for pushing me so hard during that first diagnostic meeting.) After Dr. Green did a cursory exam of my body, she looked toward my dad and asked him, "Between you, your mother, and Bethany, who would you say is the most affected?"

"I'd say my mom," he said. "She's in a wheelchair now, and she's had leg braces for the last twenty years."

"Really?" responded Dr. Green. "It seems to me, based on

what you've said, it's clear that Bethany is the worst affected. She is only fourteen, and she's already showing severe effects of CMT."

We all nodded to ourselves. She was right, clearly. I was only fourteen.

She continued, though it felt unnecessary, to elucidate the level of my decline. I had neuropathic pain; I had tremors; I had fatigue; I had muscle spasms; I had poor coordination; I had drop-foot gait; I had muscle atrophy throughout my arms and legs. And I needed leg braces.

"... and even her hands, which are usually the last to go, have visible atrophy."

"They do?" I asked.

I looked down at my hands, held them out, opening and closing my fingers to reassure myself that they still worked.

"Yes," she said. She pointed at my hands now, like a professor pointing at a diagram. "Over here," she continued, as she moved her pointer finger over the knuckles on my left hand, "you can see the wasting of your intrinsic muscles." She offered up her free hand as a "normal" specimen for comparison.

The weak intrinsic muscles were why I couldn't make a peace sign... or flip the bird.

"And if you look at your thumb," she said, pulling my thumb away from the other fingers, "you can see that the webbing here is tightening and causing a loss of thumb function."

I looked down at my fingers—trying to see what she saw, trying to see the atrophy and the disability.

But I couldn't—not yet.

6

THE SPOTLIGHT

"One, two, three, four," I counted to myself. And then I started to sing.

It was sophomore year and I was standing in front of my entire school, which—to be fair—was only 89 high school students on a good day. They sat in not *total* silence but close enough for teenagers, on the two sets of uncomfortable yellow plastic bleachers in our auditorium. I stood before them in the middle of the room: just me, a microphone, and four pages of sheet music on a wobbly black music stand.

This was my favorite thing to do—stand in front of a crowd, performing. It was a dichotomy that many people don't understand; how can a shy introvert enjoy performing in front of large crowds (the bigger the better)?

I couldn't explain to them that as desperately as I wanted to hide myself—my physical weakness—I equally craved being seen. More than that, I was desperate to connect. Performance gave me the opportunity to control how I was seen, and to be seen as I wanted to be—someone talented, bright, or otherwise valuable—and to connect without the inherent vulnerability of unscripted communication.

I had sung since I was small, sang words I didn't understand like I believed them with everything I had. When I was three I was taught to sing a long, five-minute song about winning a kewpie doll for my honey at the carnival; even then I loved the chorus of the laughter that followed, the applause, the recognition for being good.

When I found a song I loved, and that—more importantly—my audience loved, I stuck with it. I treasured the notes and their beauty. I sang only it; perfected it.

But like a child's love for a new toy, my love was fickle and fleeting. Soon I would move on to a new song, the last forgotten completely.

When I was eight, my new song of choice was "Once Upon a December," which I sang as the Grand Duchess Anastasia, re-calling distant swirling memories of my family who had been executed in Russia. I didn't know any of the context of the song at the time, and thought it was really just about dancing bears and the painted wings on a music box.

That Christmas, my grandparents gave me a plastic micro-phone and speaker set and I sang right then—as Anastasia—for my family in front of the glowing Christmas tree.

Singing was one way for me to seen, for my voice to be heard. I didn't have to worry about when to speak, or to compete for attention, or worry about if what I was saying was stupid or silly or worth anything at all.

And singing is beautiful.

One of my favorite songs to sing, the one that I was singing in front of my entire school, was from an animated children's movie called *The Snowman*.

After the heaviest snowfall that winter, a little girl builds a snowman—big and tall, and classically cute with coal buttons and an apple for a nose. That night, when the little girl should be sleeping, she sneaks downstairs to peer at her precious frozen friend through the window—and as the clock strikes twelve, she watches as he comes to life.

It is the beginning of a night full of adventures.

In the end it is very sad (spoiler: the snowman melts), but in the middle the snowman takes the girl's hand and together they fly—over towns, over forests, over the ocean. The movie has been entirely wordless until this point—until they take flight. That is when the song plays: my song, "Walking in The Air."

When I watched this movie again recently, I was surprised that there wasn't a little girl at all. It was a little boy. But I still remember her well—pale, quiet, long brown hair that wouldn't settle down. And who wanted more than anything to fly.

―――――

My eyes were closed now, one hand gripping the stand for balance. And I sang:

We're walking in the air
We're floating in the moonlit sky

The sounds of bodies shifting on uncomfortable seats ceased; the room went quiet, eyes focussed on me—just me. Singing.

―――――

After the assembly I went straight to my locker where I was followed by a group of five girls from my class. They were already chattering amongst themselves before they got to me, like a flock of small birds chirping.

I turned around to face them.

You were so amazing!
Oh my god we had no idea!
Have you been singing your whole life?
Do you take lessons?
Did you hear her????
Bethany you were INCREDIBLE!

I felt like I was flying.

————

Roughly half of the school participates in the annual school play, and there are no auditions—everyone who wants a part gets one. The drama teacher, Ms. Emery, assigned each of us our parts—based on our personalities, talents, and probably, at least a little bit, on what she thought of us.

Shortly after my debut in the auditorium, she called me up to her desk.

She didn't waste time.

"Bethany, are you doing the play again this year?" she asked.

"Yeah, I think so," I said. Although I was still a little resentful for the very small and boring part I'd had the year before (I was a dead judge who didn't get any time in court, or even a gavel), I was willing to give her another chance.

"I really hope you will," she said. "We're doing a musical, and there's a solo I think you'd be perfect for."

————

I'd heard people's lives described as "like a movie"—as if that were obviously a positive thing. Now that my life was about to be like a movie, I understood. The movie of my sophomore year would be one of those teenage flicks that your parents fall asleep to, where the heroine, who for the first half of the movie was ugly (i.e., she wore large glasses), has her shining moment where she saves the day or is otherwise seen as having some value after all—other than being the butt of a joke. She is also always discovered to be devastatingly beautiful. With her glasses gone, it's always a happy ending.

My life wasn't very much like that at all, although I did wear glasses.

But I was going to get the ending.

———

My mom hung up after her daily call with my grandmother. If women are supposed to hate their mother-in-laws, she missed the memo.

"Are they going to be there?" I asked, although I already knew the answer—my grandmother would never miss a chance to see me on stage.

That was why my mom's response surprised me.

"Well, actually, it was really strange," she said. "I asked her if she was coming to your play; she seemed surprised and said she wasn't sure that you'd want her there, because of the CMT."

"What? ...Why?"

"I don't know, she thought it might make you uncomfortable."

My mom told me that she reassured my grandmother that the idea was, of course, very, very wrong and I wanted her—both of my grandparents—there at the play, which was only two weeks away.

I didn't know why my grandmother would have thought that. Had I somehow given my grandmother the impression that I was ashamed of her? Did she think I wouldn't want my classmates to see her in a wheelchair? That was silly, since lots of grandmothers need wheelchairs.

And besides, it's not like *I* was going to end up in one.

———

A small school means low production value, so in between rehearsing my lines, I and two other girls went into an adjoining room to finish painting the backdrop for the set. Opening night was in just five days and I was putting the finishing touches of blue and white on a building's shutters. When they called me back in to run lines, I had to step carefully around the supplies strewn over the ground—paint cans, brushes, sponges, stencils, palettes.

It was during one of these trips when I felt my right leg seize up. It felt like all of the muscles in my leg decided to tighten and stay that way. This wasn't completely out of the ordinary. Over the past year I'd had similar occurrences—usually when brushing my hair—when my arm would suddenly seize up and I would be unable to move it, the hairbrush stuck mid-stroke in my hair. It only lasted a couple seconds, and I would shake out my arm and keep brushing.

I looked down at my leg—but of course nothing visible was the matter—and knowing that my two comrades were still in the room, didn't want to draw any attention to myself by acting alarmed or strange.

I attempted to shake out my stiffened leg, but instead lost my balance and arms in the air, flailing, fell backwards. Hard. On my butt.

This was in no way an "artful" fall. This wasn't a graceful cross-legged descent. This was just full-on *falling*.

"Are you okay?" I heard both of my fellow painters ask in shocked unison.

"I'm okay, I'm okay." *Besides a bruised ego and tailbone*, I thought.

They started to come over to me—stepping over art sup-plies—as I weakly tried to wave them off and save my dignity.

Then I started to realize that maybe I wasn't fine. The en-dorphins had faded now, faded enough for me to begin to feel a searing pain coming from my right leg.

I pulled my skirt back, revealing my bare knees and thighs.

My knee is gone.

That was my first thought. Except mixed with "oh god oh my god oh god."

My knee oh god my knee is gone oh my god.

It *was* gone. Sorta. Really it had just relocated. Normally a knee is round and protruding and... knee-like. Instead, where my knee should have been, my leg was sunken in like a crater. Gone! But it was only temporarily misplaced; a second later I found it off to the side of my leg. A round protruding knee where a knee did not belong.

It was grotesque.

It wasn't an inherently gross sight, not really. There was no blood or guts or pus or anything oozing out of anything else. It was gross in that way where your brain looks at something and says, "This is wrong. Very wrong. Wrong wrong wrong. ERROR. ERROR." Like when you see limbs pointed the wrong direction, or needles in eyeballs. It makes you tremendously uncomfortable and antsy and you want to look away and you feel queasy but without the urge to vomit.

That was how I felt, anyway.

"Oh! Your kneecap is dislocated. I did that once," said one of the girls in the room.

I'd heard of a kneecap dislocation before and knew that my

dad had dislocated his seven times in the last decade, events he treated the same way other dads treated a pulled muscle. No big deal, nothing to see here, this happens to everyone. But now, seeing my cratered former-knee, for the first time in my life I felt true empathy for his injuries.

The pain was beginning to intensify. Sharp blasts of pain, hacking away at my knee like a knife. A dull one. It was relentless and consuming, consuming enough that I didn't realize I had attracted a crowd in the small room full of paint supplies.

"Bethany. *Bethany!*"

It was my drama teacher, Ms. Emery. She was standing over me and, like I did with the others, I assured her I was okay— although now I knew I wasn't.

Ms. Emery wanted instructions. "Call my dad," I managed to get out. "He's done this seven times—he'll know what to do."

He told her that he would come and get me.

At some point during this time, I realized that when I had fallen I had knocked over at least two gallons of paint—yellow and blue—and I was now floating in a growing pool of it. It spread across the room, my bystanders dodging it as it approached them; my skirt soaked up what it could.

When my dad arrived, he took one look at me—lying in paint—and said, "Good God."

Apparently Ms. Emery had left out some important details, like me being covered in paint and my kneecap being dislocated.

He called an ambulance.

———

I remember the paramedics gave me morphine before moving me, and how I was momentarily grateful when I felt the needle go in, and my neural impulses forgot—for a second—the pain in my knee and instead sent signals toward the lesser pain in my arm. I also remember that they asked me how much I weighed. I lied and said I was five pounds lighter. It felt important that they not think I was fat.

The morphine lulled the pain to a quiet, constant ache, but now I needed to be moved. This was not only messy due to the paint, but tricky, since my knee needed to remain immobilized. Ultimately the paramedics opted to tie my legs together, and then no fewer than four bystanders assisted in lifting me up and over to the stretcher.

I remember my classmates' faces as I was wheeled away to the ambulance. They looked concerned, intrigued, horrified, worried, curious. Now, I'm just so glad it was before everyone had a smartphone.

———

In the corner of my hospital room was a TV set playing an ongoing football game between the University of Michigan and another team that didn't matter because it wasn't U of M. My dad pointed at the TV and said, "You and everyone who has touched you is all festive for the game."

U of M's colors are maize and blue.

I looked over at my attendings, whose once-white scrubs were now covered in blue and yellow paint from my fall an hour before.

We all laughed.

I started screaming.

My still-dislocated knee had started spasming, and the pain was no longer touched by the morphine. I screamed with every spasm, felt guilty for screaming in a pediatric ward, and kept screaming.

The nurse said they had some medicine they could give me

that would relax my muscles and stop the spasms, but that in very rare cases it can cause breathing problems and my dad would need to sign a waiver saying that in case I died, we'd been warned.

"What's it worth to you?" he said, looking at me with a smirk.

I looked at him the way you look at someone when you think maybe you really do have the hidden power to make him burst into flames.

He signed.

———

The hospital staff were anxious to get my paint-covered self out of there, so as soon as I was calm (just seconds after the medicine kicked in), they popped my kneecap back in, put the leg in a foam cast, then picked me up and lay me down across the backseat of my dad's car. They had to put down some towels first, due to the paint. My kneecap was now back in place, my leg immobilized by a large foam brace that prevented my knee from bending. On the floor of the car was a pair of crutches they had also given us, but my dad and I knew I would have neither the strength nor coordination to use them.

We drove toward home, and on the way there realized we didn't even know how we were going to get me into the house.

We came up with this: my dad would get his big leather computer chair—which was on wheels—and bring it out to the car. My dad would help pull me out and "lower" (drop) me onto the chair, while I held my leg up in the air to keep it safe. Then he would roll me (still holding onto my leg) through the garage and lift up the chair—with me in it—over the two steps to get into the house.

Neither of us knew if he had the strength to pull this off. But it worked surprisingly well (although I did scream with fear every time my leg precariously flew up into the air) until the last step.

He had successfully lifted me up over the last step (we were in the house!), when the bottom half of the chair snapped in half and I came flying—still seated—to the floor.

We couldn't help but laugh, as the picture of this was too ridiculous. But when he gave me a change of clothes and went to try to wash the paint out from my skirt, I could only sit on the floor and cry. Once again I found myself broken and on the ground.

———

I still did the play five days later, from a wheelchair. It was not the moment on stage that I'd been waiting for. It was supposed to be the climax of my life's movie, where I would shine and any thoughts of disease would be forgotten. Instead, I was stuck in this horrible metal chair with wheels and felt that the lights shown only on it, not me. How did it even matter if I sang well, if it was in a wheelchair?

Grandma watched proudly from the back row, in hers. I was so grateful that mine was only temporary.

After the play, Ms. Emery brought me—and only me—a large bouquet of red roses. She bent down a little to hand them to me, as I was still seated in my wheelchair.

Closing my eyes, I breathed in their scent, and tried to forget what had happened and where I was sitting.

7

MAY I HAVE THIS DANCE?

I grabbed the edge of our oak dining room table and pulled myself up to my feet. Balancing my weight on one foot, I pulled my nightgown over my head and threw it to the floor. I looked at the dress I was going to replace it with, draped over the table, ready for me. It was black, cocktail length, with a modest neckline and crisscross detailing which left my back partially but tastefully exposed. It was lovely and this was going to be the first time I wore it.

I slipped it over my head, pulling it and its attached slip down to just above my knees where it fell. Satisfied, I sat back down in my wheelchair with an audible *thwump*.

It was only a few weeks after my dramatic back-stage fall. I was getting ready for my high school's winter dance, despite having dropped out of high school in favor of community college a week before—just halfway through my sophomore year. My dad joked that I was his high school dropout, although in reality that wasn't how I saw myself at all—not with the bad connotations that accompany that moniker.

If anything I was proud. I thought I was a superior scholar for leaving high school early to start community college. I thought that even when my guidance counselor heard my plan and told me with certainty that if I dropped out and went to community college without a diploma or any standardized test scores, I would never be able to transfer into a good college.

Even though his harshly delivered words hurt to hear, and I had only just made it out the door before bursting into tears, I was convinced that he was wrong and didn't know anything—even if he had gone to Harvard (which he had).

It was important for me to feel like I was moving forward and keeping up with my peers—or better, outpacing them, especially as the weeks went by and I was still in a wheelchair. My knee just wasn't getting better. I spent most of my time here in the dining room; my bed had been moved next to the dining room table, since I was no longer able to get upstairs to my bedroom. It was temporary, sure—that's what I was told and knew was probably true. But I was starting to wonder if my kneecap dislocation wasn't a fluke. If maybe it was part of something bigger. Something deeper. Something related to my CMT.

My Google searches confirmed my suspicions were well founded.

incidence of patellar dislocation
risk factors for patellar dislocation
patellar dislocation charcot-marie-tooth disease
tendon and ligament involvement in charcot-marie-tooth

Even though I knew better, it was comforting to be able to explain away my wheelchair and bandaged leg to people as due to a "knee injury." *Injury.* That word was so easy, so comfortable for both myself and my listener. Way better than *I have a degenerative disease and I really don't know what's going on and my leg might be this weak forever.*

"Knee injury" brought to mind images of sports. Maybe I'd had a traumatic accident playing football, or ice hockey. But the image left me as otherwise healthy and normal. This was all temporary.

Even better, "knee injury" wasn't a lie.

What I didn't know was that I would use that explanation for years.

What happened to your leg?

Oh, I injured my knee.

Why did having a genetic disease feel so damning? Why did it feel like it said so much more about who I was as a person? That there wasn't something that had happened *to* me, but something that was fundamentally and, at its most constitutional acid-base level, wrong *with* me.

A tiny mistake, causing exponential damage.

I could still fool people and pretend that I was neurologically normal, but if I wanted to deny it to myself, that was becoming increasingly difficult to do.

Whoever said lightning never strikes the same place twice has never experienced nerve pain. The strike of lightning that had first alerted me to something going on underneath was not the last; those lightning-like pains were starting to strike more and more often—sometimes several times in the span of a minute, down an arm or a leg.

Lightning wasn't the only new sensation I was introduced to. Sometimes it felt like there were insects underneath my skin: beetles scurrying down an arm; a grasshopper hopping under the skin of my hand, causing visible movement and spasms; the butterflies with the light flapping of their wings that tingle and made me look, although nothing was ever there to explain the sensation; the bees and their sudden stings in my feet.

My wheelchair was on loan, but I had the sinking sense now that I might not be giving it back so quickly, and that it might not be the last time I used one.

I looked down at my one bare leg, a strappy sandal on its foot. My calf was thinner than I remembered it being. Could it have withered away in just four weeks of disuse?

I would be allowed to walk again in only two more weeks— but I wasn't as excited for that as I should have been. After my dislocation, we were referred to an orthopedic surgeon who told me something devastating—that I had no choice anymore, and needed leg braces.

———

I ran my fingers along the hem of my dress, which had risen up to the middle of my thighs. Leg braces meant that I wouldn't be wearing strappy sandals or this dress again; I would need to wear long pants to hide them, and wide orthopedic-looking tennis shoes to accommodate the bulky plastic braces. Shoes like my grandmother wore.

When I was a child, I assumed almost all grandmas wore leg braces. Now I realized that it was just mine.

———

This would be my first time seeing my classmates since my dramatic kneecap dislocation. Since they watched me being wheeled out on a stretcher.

My dreams often aren't in the first person but the third; I see myself outside of my body. That was how my memory of that moment was now—not from my point of view but that of my classmates'. I saw myself—broken, paint-covered—face etched with pain and humiliation.

I was now regretting my decision to attend this dance where I would have to see their faces again. At least after it was over I would never have to see them again—there was relief in that.

———

I spent the first half of the dance off to the sidelines watching my classmates dance from my wheelchair. Then I caught the eye of Laura, one of the popular and outgoing girls in my class. She was motioning for me to come in closer to join them.

I rolled my wheelchair in closer to the girls in my class, who were jumping in the air together to *Jump On It* by Sir Mix-A-Lot. Then the song changed, and Laura grabbed my hand and began dancing beside me—with me. Then another girl took my other hand, and in moments all of the girls in my class formed a spontaneous circle—and I was part of it. We danced together, all of us, with me in my chair, for the rest of the song.

I had spent the last two years desperately avoiding situations where my classmates might see there was something wrong with me. I turned down invitations, avoided stairs in groups, and on warm summer days never sat outside on the grass, because of my fear that I might not be able to get back up without help. It had never occurred to me that they might accept me for who I am. It was too late now; I would never see any of those girls again.

8

MY NEW LEGS

"A friend of mine just told me how amputees can actually do really well and run around and walk and like basically do everything, so he made me wonder why you don't think about chopping them off?" said a male relative of mine. He was referring to chopping off my legs, of course. Even though he followed up with a laugh, the laugh was followed by silence and a pointed look that suggested he actually thought this might be a good option for me.

I laughed, too, even though it wasn't very funny, and I told him that, yes, I too had seen the inspiring photos shared on Facebook of people without legs (and with prosthetics) running—but that that would not be a good option for me.

CMT is considered a "length dependent" nerve disease. Meaning that the longest nerves in my body will be affected first, and worst. The longest nerves in the body are the ones traveling from the spinal cord to the toes—and so CMT generally appears first in the feet, ankles, and calves. This leads many people to think it is a "foot disease" and that the feet are the problem. So: no feet, no problems!

Sorry, helpful amputation-happy friend—but it's not so simple. The insulation on *all* of my peripheral nerves is affected. The ones in my arm that allow me to lift and run a brush through my hair. The ones in my fingers that once allowed me to sculpt tiny doughnuts and pies. The ones in my diaphragm that allow me to breathe. The ones that allow me to sense where my body is in space. The ones that allow me to smile.

So chopping off my legs or my feet won't fix the fundamental problem: all of my wiring is shot. If I were a house, I would probably be torn down. We could cut off the parts that seem problematic, sure, but where would we stop? No matter what we do, my nerves will always have ends, and the ends will always be broken.

There are some things that can be addressed: feet that constantly trip over themselves (*"You're so clumsy!"*), ankles that twist and sprain, sores and calluses from having feet that contort and curl and don't absorb pressure across the whole foot, and a gait that is abnormal.

The primary prescription for attempting to manage these problems is leg braces.

I'd first been recommended leg braces at my diagnostic appointment when I was twelve. I was unconvinced. My parents, not seeing any urgency, and being strongly of the belief that it should be my decision, allowed me to have a private phone call with the orthotist (who would make the braces).

"It's been two weeks since I tripped, I think I'm fine"

"How many patients have you given braces to?"

"I can get them at any time, right?"

"Is there any harm in waiting?"

"I've heard that braces can make people weaker"

"I thought I read a study about an alternative treatment"

"It's my decision, right?"

I was still not persuaded after that phone call, and so the brace issue was dropped. I muddled through my daily life, tripping occasionally; falling occasionally; getting worried occasionally.

Until now, three years later, when my fall and dislocation required more visits to more doctors who told me things I didn't want to hear.

I remember the doctor—white-haired, permanent frown lines—telling me that I needed them. That, given the knee injury, I had no choice. There were no open-ended questions like "Would you like...?" or "Do you want to consider...?" At some point in the progression of my disease, I had lost the right to choose.

Which made me wonder: how long had I really had it?

Immediately after that conversation they wheeled me away—I was still in a wheelchair, five weeks in—to cast my legs for my first pair of leg braces. I knew they were my first, but I didn't know they would be the first of just so many.

At some point I must have gone to an appointment and picked them up. I must have tried them on for the first time. I say "must have," because I have no actual memory of the event.

How is that possible? I remember, so clearly, the orthotist wrapping the casting tape around my legs, encasing every inch from just below my knees.

I can remember another day, walking by our shoe rack, my old shoes waiting patiently to be worn again. I knew they wouldn't be. But I didn't grab them and toss them in the trash in a fit of fury, or create a shoe bonfire, because having them there represented that maybe there was a chance, no matter how small, that they would be worn again. To throw them away would be admitting that I had entered a new phase of my disease, a new level of loss of ability.

At some point those shoes were no longer on the shoe rack. I don't remember how that came to be, either. I know I didn't do a shoe bonfire after all, because surely that would have been unforgettable. Probably at some point when we silently all knew there was no going backwards with a degenerative disease, my mom quietly discarded them.

I remember crying in my bed at night, my pillow absorbing an endless flood of tears. When was that? Was it the first night after I first took home the braces? Or was that after our visit to the shoe store? It probably doesn't matter—they are standalone memories that don't need an exact place in a timeline to be understood.

I remember those things. But not what you'd think would be the most memorable part.

I don't remember actually receiving the braces at my next appointment. I don't remember seeing them for the first time— large, bulky, semi-opaque white plastic cocoons for my legs. I don't remember what my reaction was, or what I was thinking. I don't remember trying them on for the first time, and suddenly having a huge weight strapped to my legs. I don't remember if I noticed then how hot the plastic was, or if I realized it would make my legs break out in sweats.

It is a blank space in my timeline. It has been erased.

———

The shoe store is what I remember next, after they casted my legs for my first pair of braces.

You can't wear braces without shoes, and so that became the next step: a visit to the shoe store. This was the part I had dreaded most.

My mom and I walked into the shoe store—known for having "healthy" shoes, whatever that means—with my mom holding the braces not-so-discreetly in a thick plastic bag. Not-so-discreet because the braces were a good six inches longer than the bag.

Refusing my mom's suggestion that we speak to a salesperson first, I headed towards the displays and starting pointing out shoes that I liked—or were at least acceptable—and I believed would work. After finding five possibilities, I relented and my mom flagged over a sales guy to help us try them on.

"What do we have here?" he said, eyeing the conspicuous bag in my mother's arms.

She pulled out the braces and began explaining, while I unconsciously moved back several paces—giving myself distance from them and the conversation.

After the show-and-tell was over, I showed him the shoes I liked.

"Oh no, none of those will work," he said flatly. "They aren't wide or deep enough to accommodate the braces."

He then walked us over to a nearby shelf and plucked a pair of shoes off the display. He held them up: a pair of large, wide off-white tennis shoes with two thick velcro straps instead of laces and ventilation holes across the top and sides.

They looked just like my grandmother's.

In the closet hung the colorful skirt I had been wearing the day I'd fallen in paint and dislocated my kneecap. The paint had been washed out and it hung waiting—but I knew now that I would never wear it again.

Why is it that we can never know when we are doing some-

thing for the last time? We do with some things—a last high
school class, for example—and hope for others (a last first kiss)—
but most endings pass us by without our realizing it. At one point
I took my last jump. I skipped for the last time. I put on shoes
without leg braces. I wore a skirt for the last time. At some point,
for the last time, I looked like everybody else.

I was angry, or I wanted to be, but I had nowhere to direct
that anger. Should I be angry at my feet, my nerves? My chro-
mosomes? My body? My mind? Or could I direct it at CMT,
a disease that seemed to come from outside even as I knew it
originated deep within my genetic structure? Could I see CMT
itself as an enemy to be fought?

Not really. It wasn't an entity—something new—like a growing tumor that didn't belong there. With cancer you do have a
corporeal enemy, something that can be visualized. Attacked.
Beaten.

At first I thought of CMT that way too, but the more I read
about genetics and my disease the more false that felt. The more
my brain flashed ERROR. ERROR.

CMT wasn't an entity. CMT was me. Because what are we,
if not our genetic codes?

Where did CMT end and I begin?

There are shirts that say "FUCK CANCER!"

Somehow it didn't feel as empowering to try and find a shirt
that said "FUCK MY DNA!"

———

It was undeniable, even to me, that the leg braces improved the
way I walked. When I strode toward my first class the day after
getting my shoes, I felt a new confidence. I could *feel* that I was
walking straighter, smoother, *better*. In short, I felt like hot stuff.

And so, when I caught the eye of a fellow classmate walking toward the same building—saw him smiling and staring—I thought, *He must be thinking I look pretty damn good.*

As he got closer he said, "Hey!" followed by something unintelligible.

"What was that?" I asked, moving closer.

He repeated it. All I heard was something something leg something something.

"Sorry, what?" I said.

By this time we were both at the building, and I heard it this time.

"Did you get a new leg?"

I stood there stunned and thrown. I felt like I'd been punched in the solar plexus from the realization that he hadn't stopped me to tell me I looked good at all. I thought I was walking better than I ever had; he thought I was missing a leg.

I managed a muttered "no" before walking—actually, I guess, stumbling—away.

———

Even after that incident I was confused when one day, as I was walking down the hall, a janitor stopped and asked me, "Are you okay?"

Did I look tired? Why was she asking me that? Why was her face so concerned?

I had seen my reflection once, a reflection of someone I didn't recognize—but still didn't believe that that was what the rest of the world saw. It had been a trick of light.

I was similarly taken aback when a family friend asked me casually, out of the blue: "You must qualify for one of those dogs now, yeah?"

Or when at dinner the same family friend—staring at me eating my meal—said, "I've heard they make special spoons for crippled kids; you could try them and see if they help."

What was happening? CMT was supposed to be an "invisible disease," or at least that was the way so many people described it online, and lamented it. In fact, I had too.

But now I was being seen. And I wanted nothing more than to be invisible once again.

———

A couple months after the "new leg?" incident, I had finished my last class and was heading toward the building's front door, my school bag rolling behind me. I pressed the automatic handicap door button (a beautiful invention) and it dutifully swung open before me. But I was only halfway through the door when it betrayed me, slamming closed, knocking me down to the ground.

For someone who prided myself on learning the art of a fall, this one was—just as my kneecap-moving fall had been—not artful. In my defense, I wasn't expecting a handicap door to be moving faster than I was. I had fallen straight down, sharply onto my knees.

I crawled out of the doorway, dragging my bag behind me and sat on the ground against the outside wall of the building. Tears welled up from the particular combination of shock and embarrassment.

I still needed to find a way to get up and off the ground. After taking a couple of minutes to collect myself and let my heart rate return to normal, I took inventory of the current situation.

My knees were aching badly, although there were thankfully no outward signs of damage beyond some scrapes.

But I had no way to get up from the ground. I was too weak

and there was nothing tall enough for me to grab onto. There was nothing I could do but wait for my mom to arrive to pick me up, and with her help, try to figure out how to get me off the ground.

For the twenty minutes I sat sprawled out on the hard cement, whenever a student walked by I grabbed my bag and pretended to be rifling through it looking for something. It was imperative not to be discovered.

When my mom arrived, she didn't have much more luck getting me off the ground than I had. We were discussing our options when suddenly I was looking up at the face of a campus police officer.

"Is everything okay here?" he asked with a look of genuine concern.

My mom was in the middle of telling him how I fell and how I have trouble and we are trying to get me up and—

He reached for his walkie talkie, and yelled into it:

"WE'VE GOT A GIRL DOWN, GIRL DOWN! I NEED BACKUP, BACKUP!"

I thought backup meant a janitor coming to help pull me up. But to my surprise, when backup did arrive a few minutes later, it was in the form of two fully-uniformed officers riding up on a converted golf cart, lights flashing.

In the meantime, we had come up with the idea to grab a chair from inside the lobby, which I could use to help pull myself up. It worked and, surrounded by my mom, the three officers, and a crowd of curious onlookers, I was back on my feet.

The whole time the officers—who I figured obviously had nothing better to do—were talking loudly into their walkie talkies, declaring that they had been "dispatched" and "the situation is now under control" and "the girl is back on her feet and doing okay."

Did I mention that this was all very, very loud? Just in case anyone on campus hadn't yet heard.

———

I didn't know how anyone could possibly live with an identity wrapped up in illness and disease. Accepting it—not just internally but publicly—would, I thought, cement this illness as my identity.

It reminded me of one night when I slept over at my grandparents' house. It was late, and my grandmother walked into their home office to find me on their computer.

"What are you doing?" she asked.

"Researching CMT!" I said. I was excited about all the new information I was finding, and I was ready for her approval and enthusiasm about my embrace of our shared condition.

"You shouldn't think about that stuff too much," she said gruffly. Her face was solemn. She walked out of the office. I'd never heard that tone of voice from her.

Maybe she was right. But how could I not think about it when the world—people, my body—kept reminding me? How could I not think constantly about the fact that this body, my body, shouldn't be like this? Maybe I didn't know how a body should be, but this?

This didn't seem right.

———

During my first year at community college (I was still only fifteen and the memories of painted hospital workers and cavernous knees were still fresh), my family received a letter in the mail inviting us to a CMT conference for patients. It was being held by the national CMT Association and was close, too—just thirty minutes away, in Detroit.

My dad and I decided to go together.

But as the date came closer, my eagerness—for information, for connection—was mixed with an increasing amount of anxiety.

What would it be like to see so many people with CMT?

People who were like me?

Could there be people like me?

———

We arrived early, were greeted by friendly faces as we checked in, and sat down in the mostly empty conference room.

Out of the corner of my eye I spotted a man walking by us. He was a normal-looking guy, average, but immediately I recognized that something was different about him—something was wrong with the way he walked.

I turned and looked directly at him now, watching him walk away from us, trying to sort out what is was that was going on with him, that had jumped out at me so instantly. What had made my brain flash ERROR.

I don't think most people spend a lot of time examining the gait of others—at least I didn't at the time—looking for any peculiarities or signs of disease. But I think most of us have an innate ability to detect when someone is walking more than one standard deviation away from "normal." Walking *wrong*.

Why is this hardwired in us? Is it an evolutionary artifact from hunter-gatherer times, so we could pick out a wounded gazelle or the weakest member of another tribe? Our own tribe?

Or does it go along with the "uncanny valley" phenomenon?

Where we have, again, an innate ability to detect small deviations between a fake face and what we know a face should look like?

ERROR. ERROR.

Whatever it is, it didn't take me more than an instant to recognize that something was wrong, and only a couple more seconds to identify what.

As he walked, his legs went out too far and were lifted unusually high at the knees—as if marching, but without the straightness of a soldier. His feet were turned out and he wobbled back and forth with each step, as if he was in a constant state of unbalance.

These realizations all came first. The next realization about his walk... was that it was mine.

9

OKAY, CUPID

By the time I transferred to a four-year college two years later at age seventeen, the ever-present question, "Why did this happen to me?" had been replaced by another thought: Why *not* me? This wasn't something that had been done to me; it was one extra gene among over 20,000 others.

My grandmother lived in a tuberculosis ward for a year in her early twenties—in quarantine with other tuberculosis patients—until the doctors realized she didn't actually have tuberculosis. (Oops.) According to the family tale, the ward called her father and said that he needed to pick her up *urgently* and get her out of there. His response? "It's been a year. I doubt another day is going to hurt her."

She never did get tuberculosis, which, as a good Irish Catholic girl, she credited to the Holy Mother, Mary.

But who knows, perhaps the gene responsible for causing her own CMT also had a protective effect against tuberculosis. It wouldn't be the first time a disease-causing variant also had a protective effect.

Okay, so CMT *probably* doesn't protect against tuberculosis, but these thoughts helped to squelch the over-villainizing of a gene, and subsequently the villainization of my body. And really, we are all just one duplication or microdeletion away from tragedy. My body was doing the best it could do with what it was given. My body was not the enemy.

Slowly, without an enemy to fix on, my anger dissipated and was re-focussed into determination.

With the infinite wisdom only teenagers can possess, I decided that the best thing to do about my neurological frailty was to ignore it and continue along the life plan I had sketched out for myself.

This included transferring to Juniata College in the snowy mountains of middle-of-nowhere Pennsylvania. This may not sound like the brightest idea, but again, infinite wisdom. Juniata boasted a 100% medical school acceptance rate (actually, I think they had recently had to change that to 99.9% or something; that student must have felt really bad for ruining their statistic), and since I had ultimately given up my dream of being a princess for the more practical choice of neurologist, it made sense. Over the years, it had become clear to me that I wanted to pursue neurology as a career—if nothing else, I could give patients a better experience than the one my diagnosing neurologist Dr. Niro had given me.

Once my path to medical school was secured, I had even more urgent matters to attend to. Namely, getting a boyfriend.

My approach to romance was not so different than my approach to any other goal: getting into college, getting A's, understanding my disease.

It required diligent research and a step-by-step strategy.

Trying to date on campus was quickly eliminated as an option. Juniata was known for being a majority female college, with only 1600 students in the student body. So, with roughly 600 of them male, you can assume that at least half of those 600 are taken, and another half of those would not meet my qualifications, and another half of those who wouldn't consider me to meet *their* qualifications...

You get the picture. Pickings were slim. Add to that the fact that I didn't have the energy—or the feet—needed to socialize at parties. (At this point my feet hurt so badly when walking that I often skipped going to the cafeteria for dinner so that I would be able to make it to lab the next morning.) I also assumed—rightly or not—that the motorized wheelchair (although I preferred the term "scooter") I needed to traverse the campus might be an immediate turnoff.

I quickly settled on online dating.

I waited until my eighteenth birthday—you have to be eighteen to sign up; I would have started earlier if I could—and immediately began my research: identifying prospects, taking notes, drafting the perfect first messages.

There was one dilemma, which was how to approach my disease/disability/illness/injury/situation/what have you. I saw three options:

A. **Girl and boy meet for their first date. Surprise, wheelchair!**
B. **Girl first charms boy with her incredible personality through several messages or phone calls, and then breaks the news.**
C. **Girl says what's what on her profile.**

Option A seemed bordering on deception, and both A or B offered the risk of to-my-face rejection.

And so I chose option C. Of course this meant many potential suitors could disqualify me immediately, but… so what? I had to make that be okay in order to survive this already rejection-centric process. I knew intellectually that it would be difficult to date someone with a disease/disability/illness/injury/situation/ what have you, and I also knew that people dismiss partners for much sillier reasons like bad taste in music or literature. It wasn't personal, I told myself. Just… preferences! That said, I preferred to avoid direct face-to-face rejection, opting instead for a process that wouldn't let me know if I'd been cast aside or not.

I went for a carefully crafted two sentences in my profile— under the category *The Most Private Thing I'm Willing To Admit*: "I have a neuromuscular disease and use a scooter to get between buildings on campus. But it hasn't stopped me from living an awesome and full life."

And there was definitely a smiley face at the end. To show that I'm super cool with it.

:-)

On December 7, less than two weeks into my search, I logged on and a new match popped up on the front page.

Username: sinclair44
Match percentage: 87%
Enemy percentage: 7%
Age: 20
Location: Pittsburgh, PA
Photo: Wearing a top hat; cute

Click.

———

sinclair44's profile was both unusually well-written and long, especially considering it said he had signed up for the site that day.

I sent him a message immediately. Four carefully chosen sentences, one emoticon.

When I woke up the next morning at 6:30 for my Invertebrate Zoology lab, the first thing I did was check my messages.

He had responded. Score.

His response was seven paragraphs long. And he had upped the emoticon game to four.

It ended with:

How long do these responses typically go on? If writing a 3000 character essay in response to a simple question is overly excessive, please excuse me since I haven't really done this very much at all. :)

Curious to hear from you!

Josh

———

"I'd love to hear more about type theory," I found myself saying—or rather, typing—to Josh after hours of messaging back and forth over a period of a few days.

This was not true. Although it was true that I was interested in hearing him talk—actually talk, hear his voice on the phone for the first time—even if it was about something as boring as type theory probably was.

And so we agreed to have a call—later—giving me enough time to first read the Wikipedia article on type theory so I could come prepared with an intelligent question. (It worked, by the

way, prompting the response, "That's a really good question, and
there is a lot of debate...")

That first call lasted only five minutes, which was good since
I only had one question prepared. My parents got home just after
Josh had explained the intricacies of the type theory debate; I
didn't want to listen to my dad making fun of me, so I hung
up before my parents could hear me say, "Oh, fascinating, wow,
never thought of infinite recursion that way!"

I was home for winter break now, and just a few days prior—
about a week after I sent Josh that first message—I had been in
the process of sitting down on the toilet when I felt my kneecap
pop out and back into place. (Why is it never something digni-
fied?)

And so for the second time my bed was brought down to the
dining room where I would spend the entirety of my days while
my knee healed. Having my potential suitor to talk to online
made the fact that I couldn't walk easier to handle, although it
would have been nice to have a little more privacy.

———

One night, not long after my introduction to type theory, Josh
and I were up late messaging each other and our parents had
long since gone to bed.

This was the opportunity to have a real conversation on the
phone.

We stayed up all night talking—about ourselves and our answers to the weird dating site questions and how much funnier
fortune cookie fortunes are if you add "...while I watch" to the
end of them.

We talked until 6:30 in the morning. And all night again the
next day. And the next.

We were both clearly enamored by each other, and I didn't want our calls or our conversations to end. But my happiness was short-lived, as it was after one of these long calls that he sent the message I'd been dreading:

"There's something I've been meaning to ask you."

But—he said—he was too tired now; it would have to wait until tomorrow.

I knew what he wanted to ask me. I'd been waiting for it the entire time. Honestly, I was surprised it hadn't come sooner. Extra honestly, it had been really fun to not even have to address it.

He was finally going to ask me about my disease/disability/illness/injury/situation/what have you. He was going to ask, essentially, *"So, how disabled are you?"*

I went to bed that night dreading The Question. I went through the imaginary conversation in my head twenty different times and twenty different ways. Had I just been kidding myself that this was something a twenty-year-old could look past?

My plan to minimize rejection was not looking so great.

———

THE FOLLOWING EVENING

Josh has signed on.

BETHANY: So what was it you wanted to ask me?
JOSH: Oh, yeah...

Josh is typing...

[three painful minutes elapse]

Finally he hit "send" on the novel he had apparently been composing. The Question had finally come, in the form of a very long, obviously nervous, and semi-rambling paragraph. The only part that mattered to me was this:

"Would you like to go on a date with me?"

We set our first date for January 23, 2010, when we would both be back in school from winter break, and my knee would be all healed up. Otherwise our first date would have had to be in my kitchen, which didn't seem a thousand percent ideal for budding romance. The plan was that Josh would take the three-hour train ride from his college, Carnegie Mellon, in Pittsburgh, to Juniata College in Huntingdon, Pennsylvania, and we would... see what happened.

He set a countdown on his computer and we started counting down the days.

The morning of our date I tried to distract myself with articles and games on the computer—even homework—to avoid worrying about the impending visit. But it was impossible to forget, especially as Josh sent periodic updates ("T minus 4 hours!" "At the train station!") and our countdown changed from hours to minutes. I changed shirts three times, settling on one with the pi symbol (sure to woo a computer science/physics double major). I paced around the room—mentally. I brushed my hair, which didn't need brushing.

JOSH: ETA 5 minutes!

JOSH: I'm wearing a green jacket.

Sure enough, a couple minutes later I saw a guy wearing a green jacket walking up the hill toward my dorm. I watched him, waiting for him to see me, shifting my weight back and forth nervously. I saw him look in my direction—surely he had seen me—I was standing outside the front door—but then he looked away and kept walking. Past me and my building.

My heart dropped. Had he really taken one look at me and suddenly changed his mind? Was I standing funny? Or just that ugly?

These were the horrible thoughts running through my head when I saw a second guy coming up the hill toward me.

He was wearing a green jacket.

It was him.

He was out of breath by the time he reached me as he had jogged most of the way from the train station to maximize our time together.

First dates are awkward enough even when they aren't so anticipated. When I invited him into my room he commented that he'd forgotten to hug me, although as he went in for a greeting-hug, he simultaneously apologized for being sweaty due to sprinting to my dorm; I didn't hold on too long so he wouldn't feel self-conscious.

We sat on my bed (it was a dorm room, I didn't have guest seating), and he pulled out a card game he had promised to bring. The bed would have to serve as table and chairs for this welcome ice breaker.

But before we began the game, I needed to take my shoes and braces off. As my feet began to curl more due to the CMT, wearing the leg braces had become progressively painful, and often left my feet covered in bulging sores and blisters. To minimize this and to be able to concentrate on anything at all, I had to remove them as soon as I sat down.

I didn't let anyone see my braces other than my parents and the orthotist who made these plastic legs, and a guy I liked and was on a first date with was not going to be the first exception. I couldn't very well say, "Please turn around while I take off my leg braces," though, could I?

With him sitting a couple feet from me on the bed, I tried to take them off as covertly as I could, back turned. As soon as they were off my legs, I shoved them underneath the bed.

I could sense him lean forward and peer at what I was doing, but he didn't ask or say anything.

—

After I won the card game (it wasn't even close), we agreed to go to one of the campus restaurants for lunch. He waited for me as I got into my wheelchair scooter, held the door as I zoomed out of it, and walked alongside me over to the dining hall.

I parked my scooter and together we walked into the dining hall, him taking my hand into his.

10

HOLDING HANDS

I spent most of my time at college in my dorm room, in front of my computer sitting on the wooden "rocking chair" that came with the room. I put rocking chair in quotes because it only had two states: upright or flung back. That was where I was—clicking at nothing in particular—when I got the call. It was my mom.

"Honey, I'm so sorry to tell you but you need to know: Grandma May is dying."

I needed to come home. Now.

My mom told me that my cousin and his girlfriend were driving from New York to Ann Arbor and would pick me up on the way. They would be here tonight (it was already "night" by most standards).

I threw some toiletries and clothes—one set black—in a bag.

———

Grandma was the first person I called after my first date with Josh. Grandma was always overly protective of me, so I was a little surprised by how calm and happy she seemed to be when I told her I went on a date with a boy—a boy I'd met on the internet.

It was only later that I learned she was only calm with me,

and one by one she called her children to ask them what they thought, what to do, and to stalk this boy on "the Face Book" and report their findings back to her.

———

We arrived at the hospital and I immediately saw my mom running towards me. With a tight hug, she said, "Bethany, there are two things you need to know before you see her." She held me now at arm's length, and her faced turned serious. "She may not recognize you, and it's the CMT that is killing her."

———

My usually sensitive mother apologized later for the lack of tact in her delivery, and for my part I choose to believe that my grandmother did recognize me—that she knew it was me holding her hand as she lay dying.

This is what I need to believe, especially after my aunt told me that the day before I had arrived she'd been moaning softly, "Where's my Bethany? Where's my Bethany?"

———

I remembered how she used to grab my hands in hers as a child— tender, stroking them—telling me how young and beautiful and perfect mine were.

They were young and beautiful and perfect, although now I wonder if even then she could detect the same frailties in mine that had affected hers.

I could see my frailty now—the one a doctor had pointed out four years before. I could see it plainly. The thinning of my hands and wrists. How my fingers didn't want to straighten and tried to stay curled. The awkwardness with how I picked up a spoon or held a pencil. I had started to avoid raising my hand in class for the fear that others could see it too.

That touch is so vivid. Tender, but not soft—she held them tight as if she were afraid of what would happen if she let go.

Why didn't I tell her then that I thought her hands were perfect, too? They weren't young like mine—the skin was soft and loose, with an almost translucent quality. Blue veins bulged out from a lack of muscle tone.

But they were Grandma's hands. They were the hands that made me mashed potatoes, that handed me cards under the table if I was losing at a game (even as I reached an age where this should have been embarrassing), the hands that rubbed my back to help me fall asleep. The hands that clutched mine so fervently.

"Your beautiful hands. So young and beautiful."

After visiting Grandma in the hospital, I went to my grandparents' house to spend the night. I didn't know that I would be sleeping in my grandparents' bedroom.

When I walked into their room, it was still. Her leg braces stood by the bed, waiting for an owner who would never return.

I took my shoes and leg braces off and stood them beside hers.

I slipped in on her side of the bed, pulled my legs up to my chest and thought about how she had lain here every night for over forty years.

She wasn't gone yet—although it was a matter of days, maybe even hours—but it was too late now to have the conversations I wished we could have, to ask the questions I wished I had had the courage to ask.

My grandmother and I barely ever talked about CMT. But there was one time when I saw her struggling to open a can of soda and said, "I have trouble with that too."

Then she asked me if sometimes my hands cramp, if sometimes they give out, and if I had trouble with stuff like getting dressed or opening jars of peanut butter.

Of course every answer was affirmative—we shared part of the same world.

It was a short conversation, a couple of minutes. But I know it was meaningful because I so clearly remember her reaction. It wasn't joy—certainly she wouldn't feel joy for me struggling—but it was a warmth. To know that someone understood a painful, private, constant struggle, and for a brief moment to be able to have that shared understanding. Yes, that chromosomal defect had given me an error code. But it also gave me a link to Grandma, a tie that the two of us knew ran through our blood and our DNA, a connection that transcended even the already-strong bonds of family. We were in this together, even if we couldn't ever directly see what "this" was.

———

A few years before she died, Grandma had asked me to promise I would sing Ave Maria, her favorite song, at her funeral. I told her yes, of course Grandma, and we quickly moved on to less morbid conversation.

Ave Maria is a technically difficult song with very high notes, and I knew that I would not be able to sing it at her funeral like she had asked me to. When she had seen me sing before, I was still able to take deep enough breaths to get those notes out; now, the CMT had weakened the nerves around my diaphragm as well as the more obvious ones around my feet and hands. CMT was starting to affect even interests that don't seem overtly physical; of course, once the body starts failing, they all do.

I wished I could tell her I was sorry—to ask if maybe she could ask for a different, less difficult song—but she could no longer speak.

————

With the type of CMT that runs in my family, there is a 50% chance that each child will have CMT. It is a coin flip with every pregnancy.

My grandparents had four children, and so the coin was flipped four times. If the CMT gene is "tails," then the flips went:

Child #1: Heads
Child #2: Heads
Child #3: Heads
Child #4: Tails

My dad, the youngest, was the only one who ended up getting the disease.

People like to say things like, "You have your father's nose" or "I see your grandfather's dimple on you," but we don't *really* know where those genes came from. With CMT, I do. I have my grandmother's gene, passed through my father and then on to me.

It's a little piece of her, and proof that there must be other little pieces of her in me, too.

————

"Isn't she beautiful?" my grandfather said, wrapping an arm around me as we stood alone together in front of her open casket.

"She is."

———

My father gave the eulogy at Grandma's funeral. In his eulogy, he spoke of a mother's love.

Sometimes when a person is remembered, it is said of that person that she put her family first. However, to say that Mom put her family first would be misleading. Because first implies that there is a second, and a third. Mom had a special calling, a special gift, and as a result she did not have to divide her attention as we do. Mom's calling, her vocation, was mothering.

———

What are we if not our bodies? Our bodies allow us to communicate with and to experience the world; our bodies are what finally decide when our time is up; and at the end, our bodies are what is left of us. Death is all about the body, and yet this encounter with it made me worry a little less about how a body should be, and more about how a person should be.

———

Mom's love, however, was not without limits, and it did not extend to the large black birds that she called Grackles. If you want to see Mom's fury, do one of two things: Tell her that a Grackle is eating from her bird feeder. Or criticize a grandchild.

Grandma couldn't protect me from the Grackles in our family tree—although she tried. In the end, she could only hold my hand, and I hers.

11

CUT ALONG THE DOTTED LINE

Josh was under the impression that I was recovering from another "knee injury"—that pushing his eighteen-year-old girlfriend around in a wheelchair and helping her walk to the bathroom at night was temporary. After I recovered, I'd be better. Not "normal"—I did have CMT, whatever that meant—but back to how I'd been before.

And how I was before this last kneecap dislocation seemed, now, from this vantage point, gloriously able. Before, I could at least stand and walk around my dorm room without my leg braces. Not anymore. As soon as I tried to stand on bare feet, my ankles turned out and I crumpled to the ground.

This development made everything dramatically more difficult. For example, showering. The communal showers in my girls' dorm were literally across the hall from my room. This meant that, before, I could take off my braces in my room, carefully walk the few yards over to the shower, strip down, shower, walk back.

Now, unable to stand without my braces, that meant I had to leave them (and my tennis shoes) on while in the shower. This presents an obvious problem: dripping wet tennis shoes, the only pair of shoes I could wear. Not to mention the horror of traipsing around my dorm in a nightgown and visible leg braces.

There were some months where I went over a week without showering out of fear or exhaustion at the whole process.

When I visited Josh in Pittsburgh, everywhere we went had to be calculated for accessibility. Staying in wasn't much easier. He shared a house off campus with three other students, and his room was up two long flights of steep stairs. I had to bend over and use my hands to help get me up, grabbing onto each dust-covered step. Sometimes I had to crawl and rest on the stairs several times to catch my breath.

I wasn't purposely deceptive with Josh (no more than he was when he let me win that card game on our first date, a fact he admitted years later), because I was under the same delusion. That this was temporary. That I would get better.

And, if I accidentally misled him as I misled myself, I knew that Josh wouldn't just go along with things because he thought it was too hard to call it quits. You don't rush Josh into anything; when I told him I loved him for the first time—a few weeks after my grandmother's death—he waited a whole entire week before whispering in my ear: "I've been thinking a lot, and I've come to the conclusion that I love you too."

———

The orthopedic surgeon held up each of my feet in front of him, bending them up, down, left, right. We were here because when I returned back to my beloved physical therapist that summer after a difficult year at Juniata and told her I wanted (and expected) her to get me walking again, she soon told me that it was not going to happen, my feet were too far gone, and it was time to see a surgeon if I wanted to walk again.

When my parents wheeled me into the surgeon's office, I knew he would tell me I needed surgery. I was an eighteen-year-old in a wheelchair, plus, what surgeon tells you you *don't* need surgery? I knew what procedures he would almost certainly recommend (I knew how to Google), which were tendon transfers for both feet. The tendon transfers would balance out my feet again and allow them to lay flat, instead of the contorted mess they had turned themselves into.

After a minute of quietly communing with my feet, he announced—to no one's surprise—that I did need surgery, and—to everyone's surprise—that it would involve ten surgical procedures *per foot.*

10 + 10 = 20

20 procedures.

Not only would this include the anticipated tendon transfers, but cutting and rearranging bones, and slicing as far up as my mid-calf.

———

After the appointment, my parents observed that the surgeon was incredibly good-looking—like he should be a character on Grey's Anatomy. I hadn't noticed. It is hard for someone to be attractive when he also seems really enthusiastic about cutting you open. Twenty times. So while they were frothing at the mouth about his cheekbones and sharp eyes, all I could find to say about him was that he was, quite possibly, a sadist.

We went to a second surgeon for a second opinion. I was hoping the second opinion would be a different opinion, but it was not.

10 + 10 = 20.

Unlike the first surgeon, who said I would need the surgeries "within ten to fifteen years," this surgeon took a harder stance. He told me unequivocally that he thought I needed these surgeries *now*, that they could not wait. And he told me unequivocally the horrors that would be involved, saying ruefully that I would hate whoever did this to me for a long time. But even as he gripped my big toe between his thumb and forefinger and described how the first thing he would do is break it, I *liked* him. "We are going to destroy your feet," he said. I looked at him. Pause. "And then, we are going to rebuild them." I exhaled.

I liked him because he was the first person who saw an eighteen-year-old being wheeled into his office and made it clear he thought that was unacceptable, wanted better for me, and was confident that he knew how to help.

———

When I was two years old, I was wobbling past the bottom of the staircase in our new home when a distant relative tripped and tumbled down several stairs. Unharmed but startled, she sat at the bottom of the stairs. I stared at her, quiet. I had a messy mop of dark brown curls, and looked like a miniature brunette version of Shirley Temple.

"Are you going to come comfort me, little Bethany?" she asked.

"Who said life is fair?" I replied. Then I toddler-wobbled away.

I now realize that "Who said life is fair?" is an inappropriate response to someone falling down the stairs. However, in my defense at the time, I was merely repeating a phrase that my grandfather had devilishly taught and coached me to say. Although the timing was inappropriate, I think my grandpa was secretly delighted to learn his hard work had paid off. The message was sinking in. Life isn't fair. And I was growing to be proof.

I believed that the only way to deal with this fact was to continue plowing ahead and not let life's circumstances get in the way or slow me down. I would have to take a year off from school in order to get these surgeries—and that would mean altering my plans because of my disease. It made me wonder: if I started doing that now, at eighteen, what could it mean for the rest of my life? Was CMT going to dictate every step? Although I hadn't voiced it yet, I was already worried about how I would have the energy or the physical capabilities to get through med school and residency—but to contemplate alternatives would mean giving up on my dreams because of this, and that seemed like the worst thing I could do to myself.

I had to take a stand now. I had to finish school even if I couldn't stand by the end of it. To give in now could lead to everything crumbling. To give in now would mean that there really was something terribly wrong with my body. To give in now would mean that I was fundamentally broken, somewhere deep inside. That this wasn't just something layered on top of a disease that could be treated. That this meant that the body, *my* body, wasn't as it should be.

And so even though Second Opinion Guy had made a solid case, I still decided to put off the surgeries. I had a plan, and the next step in that plan was to graduate at twenty.

———

Two weeks before the new semester, I was attempting to climb a staircase in Josh's childhood home, but my ankles kept rolling outward and I kept falling toward each step. I attempted to balance myself by bending forward with one arm bracing myself on the railing, and the other grabbing onto the next step in front of me. I might have found my pose comical (it was), were it not for the fear that on the next step one of my legs might give out completely and I would come tumbling down the stairs. The amount of walking I could do had continued to decline that summer, and each step I did take was taking a painful toll.

I did end up crumpling onto that staircase, but not because my leg had given out—*I* had. I couldn't stand it any longer, and I sat on that staircase and cried. I cried for my body, for everything I'd lost, and I cried because I knew what I needed to do.

That week I told my college I was taking a year off for medical leave, and we scheduled my first surgery for the following month.

———

Right before they wheeled me into the operating room, my surgeon (the possibly very handsome possible sadist) stopped in to say his hellos and relax us with his always calm presence. He picked up my left leg and began drawing dashed lines all over the foot, ankle, and calf—like the kind you see on packaging with a little scissors symbol next to it and the words "Cut Here."

I'm not sure which thought is worse: that your surgeon needs guidelines to remember where to cut, or that he might freehand it and accidentally operate on the wrong foot.

Yeah, I'm okay with the lines.

After the lines were drawn, my mom—who always had her camera at the ready—prompted my surgeon and me to smile for a photo together.

I have that photo now, and I think my smile looks a little forced.

Whenever I protested at her taking photos of me during the

surgery process, she would always say, "It's for the memory!" In my opinion, there are some memories you don't want to keep.

———

It was around then that my dad started referring to my surgeon as "God." Because, he said, "He makes people walk again, just like Jesus." And he did have some God-like qualities. For example, the nurses told us right before surgery that they really liked him because he didn't swear and yell at them in the operating room. (There was an implication that this was not the case with the other surgeons there.)

And we had to have faith in him, not dissimilar to one's faith in God. We had to have faith that he would make me walk (really walk) again.

Maybe my dad also found it more comforting, as my parents waited together for the four-hour surgery, to say that God (who happened to be very handsome) was performing the surgery. Surely that would be more comforting than admitting that "God" was just a person, cutting into his daughter, trying to piece her back together again.

Piece her back together better than she had been before.

———

Bethany is the name of a town in the Bible. According to accounts in the New Testament, Bethany was home to an almshouse for the poor and the sick, and one of its inhabitants was Lazarus. According to the story, Jesus receives word that Lazarus is very ill, but takes his time getting to him, and by the time he arrives Lazarus is very dead. Super dead. If the story ended there it would not be an especially good story, but luckily, after Jesus has been thoroughly chastised for being late, he goes straight to

Lazarus's tomb and raises him from the dead.

So that's one thing Bethany—the town—has going for it.

But Bethany—the name—has some less than great connotations. A lot of websites list the meaning of Bethany as either "house of dates" or "house of figs." Not exactly the coolest meaning (Sarah means princess; Diana means heavenly)—but also, at least, fairly inoffensive.

There are scholars who spend their lives studying all sorts of things, and some of them have spent years arguing and writing about what they think are the true meanings of Bethany. And they have put forward substantial cases for alternative meanings of Bethany:

"House of poverty."
"House of affliction."
"House of misery."

————

What was supposed to be three days of recovery in the hospital turned into two weeks.

This is a little of what that was like:

Pills that make the pain go away, pills that don't make the pain go away, pills that make you hallucinate your mother hitting you with a chicken (roasted, not live), opioid induced constipation, opioid withdrawal, being told you need more opiates, not being allowed to bathe yourself, lots of people seeing you naked, swelling in weird places, being woken up every few hours at night by nurses who want to check your perfectly normal blood pressure, learning why mothers rave about epidurals (when your idiot anesthesiologist pulls your morphine drip too soon), IVs, more IVs, greasy hair, the smell of excrement from your adult roommate's diaper changes, pain, pain, pain, not being allowed to leave, wanting desperately to leave, spending almost all hours of the day in your hospital bed, regretting your life choices that led to you being in said hospital bed, your catheter being your new (always reliable) best friend, wondering if maybe your mother really did hit you with a chicken, doctors who always believe your chart over you, your chart being wrong, feeling alone.

————

There were some things to look forward to during the long days in the hospital, and that was the cards. Every day my mom would bring in a new handful of get well cards from family and friends. Occasionally, there were also presents!

One such present arrived in the form of a large brown box, at least three feet high. It was signed "Love, Grandma Dorothy," my mom's mom. As I set to work on the box, my mom forewarned: "Your Grandma was really excited to get this for you. I guess it's a collectible. But then she realized it might be a little young for you."

A few minutes later, my attempt to open the box futile, my mom grabbed it from me and opened its flaps to reveal the contents.

It was a bear.

A massive, white, stuffed bear with a pink bonnet and bow around its neck.

I couldn't help but laugh. Even with the warning, it wasn't exactly what I had expected! But wait, there was more. Knowingly, my mom pressed its right paw and the bear comically bopped back and forth, its fuzzy lips mouthing the words to a heavily compressed version of a country tune.

It was cute, I admit. Unintentionally hilarious, but cute. However, the bear rapidly became less cute as, unfailingly, every person who entered my room insisted on having the bear sing its song.

All of the nurses on the floor were obsessed with the bear. My dad thought this was hilarious, and would press its paw whenever he saw a moment to get a reaction out of me.

One morning my dad walked into my room, greeting me while making a beeline for the bear.

"Oh come on, not again" I whined. I was irritable, having been woken again at 4 a.m. the night before (110/70, if you were wondering).

"It's adorable!"

The bear was singing now.

"Hey, what's it saying?" my dad asked.

I sighed, and with as little enthusiasm as possible sang along with the bear:

May you climb the tallest mountain,
And sail the deepest sea.
'Cause you're just getting started
And the best is yet to be.

The best is yet to be.

———

When my surgeon unveiled my new foot for the first time, several weeks post-op and the horrors of the hospital tucked away deep in my mind, I was in awe. It was the most beautiful foot I'd ever seen. It didn't actually *look* beautiful yet; it was admittedly kind of ugly, swollen, multi-colored, bruised—covered in ghastly incisions and dried blood (we nicknamed it Frankenfoot). But it was beautiful to me because it was straight, the way a foot should be—the way it had used to be.

The first thing I did after admiring its beautiful ugliness—and pose for pictures with it (more memories)—was count the incisions and ask what each one was for. The counting became a habit every time I got to see my foot.

One, two, three, four, five, six, seven, eight.

At some point during the process of surgery, there had been a shift in how I thought about and referred to my feet. They were no longer "my feet" or "my foot" but "the feet" or "the foot." This distancing is probably some type of protective mechanism. It wasn't me being cut into—it was the feet. It wasn't me hurting—it was the feet.

The distancing didn't make me care less about them—the feet. If anything I became almost *motherly* toward them. Counting those incisions over and over—making sure everything was as I left it, as it should be.

———

It wasn't until several months later—after the whole process had been repeated—that I got to see my other foot in its new Franken beauty. As soon as he'd removed the cast and I'd let out a breath after seeing that it, too, was the pinnacle of perfection, I began counting the incisions. I knew they would be the same, but I still counted.

One, two, three, four, five, six, seven, eight, nine... wait, what? I counted again. Nine.

"Um," I said to my surgeon. "Why are there nine incisions when there were only eight on the other foot?"

"There aren't," he said. "They are the same."

"Look…" I counted for him now, pointing to my healed left foot. "One, two, three, four, five, six, seven, eight. But on this one…" I turned back toward my right foot, "One, two, three, four, five, six, seven, eight, *nine*."

"Huh," was his first response. Not exactly confidence boosting. "I guess I decided to go in differently on this one."

Ultimately, the surgeon hadn't done anything bad or crazy, but that was the moment that I realized I didn't really *know* what had been done to my body. I had the *illusion* of knowing and of control—but I didn't really. Even when it was explained, there were facts, decisions, choices that were left out. What really happened after I was under and the curtain was pulled? Was there even a curtain or was it just a door?

Counting to eight or to nine was no longer enough. I needed to know what each of those incisions-turning-scars meant.

———

I didn't feel better when I saw the x-rays of both of my new feet. That was how I saw their new hardware for the first time: a plate in the bone connecting to each big toe—two little screws holding them together—and two impossibly large screws in each heel bone.

Plates: 2
Screws: 8

He wasn't a God. He didn't have the parts to destroy and rebuild me from scratch. And yet he had.

———

At one of my follow-up appointments I finally asked my surgeon for copies of my operative reports. I thought maybe this would give me a sense of clarity, an understanding of what exactly had been done while I'd been out. Maybe it would help me parent my feet better, to see what they had gone through. He had the surgical reports printed for me at the end of the appointment and I left clutching the pages—two papers, one per foot.

For the first time I saw the names of all of the procedures. I could begin to match them up to the incisions I'd counted repetitively.

First metatarsal osteotomy
Calcaneal osteotomy
Tarsal tunnel release
Gastrocnemius release
Flexor digitorum longus tendon transfer
Posterior tibialis tendon transfer
Plantar fascia release
Ankle ligament repair

And I could read, step by step, what had happened during those periods I couldn't remember.

"The osteotomy was performed with an oscillating saw..."

12

MR. RIGHT

"What's wrong?" my mom asked as she walked through my bedroom. Well, "bedroom." It was actually the dining room, where my bed had been for the past four months and would remain until I could reliably walk up the stairs to my real room. I missed my room. I had redecorated it just before leaving for college; I couldn't decide on a paint color, so we ended up painting one wall yellow, one green, one teal, and one white. (I wouldn't want it to be over-the-top.)

I've been told I have an expressive face and am easy to read. If that is the case, my face would have read anger.

"He should be here this weekend," I said.

"I know you miss him," said my mom, while opening the refrigerator.

"It's our one year anniversary tomorrow."

The anniversary of our first date was an important milestone, and I was still fuming after a conversation I'd had with Josh over messenger that went like this:

> **BETHANY: What are your plans this weekend?**
> **JOSH: Not much going on for once.**

BETHANY: So can you come visit me?

JOSH: It's too late to buy train tickets. Too bad, this
would have been a good weekend to visit
it turns out.

BETHANY: ...

Maybe this doesn't seem that worth getting angry over, but when you've been stuck spending all hours of the day in the dining room—with its four painfully dull white walls that you literally cannot walk away from—every little injustice that you suffer seems greater. It wasn't like he was doing anything important, other than taking several courses in computer science and physics whose paragraph-long course descriptions were completely incomprehensible.

———

I saw Josh in my dreams that night. He was sitting on the edge of my bed, looking down at me and smiling.

"Bethany, look who's here." It was my mother speaking, and then as Josh took my hand I realized that it wasn't a dream.

Josh had taken an overnight train to come see me. He had arrived at our train station at 4 a.m. where my dad picked him up. (I found out later that this surprise trip had been planned for weeks.)

Now he was sitting beside me, just smiling and holding my hand.

"Are you really here?" I asked.

"I'm here," he said. "Happy anniversary."

I grabbed him now, and we hugged each other tightly while I cried.

"Why did you make me get so mad at you?" I said.

He smiled. "I can't *make you* do anything."

———

I wish recovery were more like some religious miracle and less like what it was. "And then she walked again! Hallelujah!" would be the miracle version. "This hurts," was the real one.

There was no singular hallelujah moment where I went from not walking to walking. No moment where tears were shed at the miracle.

Instead, recovery was a very long series of mostly boring, seemingly un-monumental moments.

Recovery was a series of casts and lying on that bed in the dining room with its white walls. It was then, finally, moving into a "walking boot," which it turns out is a misnomer, since it was almost impossible to walk in.

It was unending physical therapy—three times a week every week—where I pointed my foot, and flexed my foot, and pointed my foot, and flexed my foot, BUT DON'T MOVE IT IN THAT DIRECTION OR YOU'LL UNDO THE SURGERIES, and pointed my—

Even though there was no hallelujah Hallmark moment (the kind that goes viral on Facebook), there were small but meaningful victories during the rest of my recovery. Being able to walk to the bathroom at night barefoot, without the long process of first putting on my leg braces and shoes. Showering without tennis shoes, as God intended. The first time I realized that it no longer hurt to walk.

———

Josh and I walked hand-in-hand to the Dairy Queen near my house—a whole 0.8 miles away, and another 0.8 miles back.

It was the first time I'd been able to walk there since I was small. Or at least that's what I guessed; it was so long ago that I couldn't actually remember a time when I could walk that distance. I still needed my leg braces for leaving the house—the surgeries hadn't fixed that—but they had given me back so much that I couldn't complain. I wasn't greedy.

New abilities did bring me new problems. I didn't realize— or had forgotten—what it was like to walk during a Michigan summer.

"I'm sooo hot," I said, panting for dramatic effect.

"You should wear shorts," said Josh.

(Josh always has helpful solutions.)

"I don't wear shorts," I said.

"Why not?"

I sighed. "Because."

"Because what?"

"Because of my braces."

No matter how I tried to explain why *obviously* I did not want to and could not wear shorts with leg braces, I kept being met with "But why?" or "So?" or "Who cares?" or "You'd be a lot less hot in shorts."

It was infuriating.

———

A couple weeks before I was due to return to Juniata, I made another huge decision. Realizing that there was nothing honorable about being totally miserable, which pursuing medical school was starting to look like, I let go of that plan. It was time to make a new one, one that was maybe against my original script, but at the same time, still totally *mine*.

This new plan had me moving to California, where there would be no ice or snow (treacherous, wretched things), and where I could live with relatives and have access to physical therapy. It was easier to decide to divert my path this time, since previously letting go of my fierce hold on "the plan" in order to have surgeries had given me back something I thought was gone forever. CMT is a progressive disease—no one talks about "getting better" or improving—but I had.

The only negatives were that I would need to reapply to colleges, and that my dad teased me relentlessly about how I was "following a boy around the world." (Josh had just graduated and also happened to be moving to Silicon Valley to work as a software engineer.)

———

Over the years I'd had several family members commiserate with me over my struggles with braces and fashion. They had helped me try to come up with ways to hide or disguise my braces— bootcut jeans, bellbottoms, long skirts, leg warmers.

But I couldn't remember any of them ever suggesting I just let them be seen.

And I definitely had never met anyone who reacted as Josh did—which seemed to be a fundamental incapability of understanding *why* I would possibly need to hide them. It just did not compute for him.

At first his reactions were frustrating and seemed unempathetic. He just *did not get it.* But each time we had the same conversation ("I'm hot." "Wear shorts." "I can't." "Why not?") it started to seep into my own way of thinking about myself.

Why not?

I knew the answer. I felt embarrassed of my leg braces. Ashamed.

Why?

I was scared of the world seeing me as I saw myself; that they would judge me as harshly as I judged myself.

Because I was really embarrassed of myself, of my body, of my disability.

But again:

Why?

———

It would have been easy if turning off a fear were as easy as flipping a switch. Instead, it usually involves confronting the fear head-on and—hopefully—it isn't as bad as you thought it would be.

I went to Target and picked out a pair of shorts from the juniors' section. They were pale blue with a pink floral print and deliberately frayed bottom. And they were short.

At nineteen, they were still more-or-less age appropriate, but I wasn't shopping for my nineteen-year-old self—I was shopping for the girl in high school who never had the courage to wear cute shorts like the other girls in her class.

The shorts sat in my drawer, untouched, for a few weeks. Until one day I stood up, took off my jeans, slipped on the shorts, and walked out of the house.

I kept walking down the sidewalk and all the way to the busy downtown streets. I walked up and down the sidewalk past strangers talking on their smartphones, past families trying to hold onto their small children, young women holding armfuls of shopping bags strolling in and out of little boutiques, past restaurant and shop vendors trying to grab the attention of the chronically inattentive. I walked until I grew tired, and then I sat on a bench on the edge of the sidewalk. I watched them walking by me, looking at their faces—searching them—but they weren't looking at me at all.

I was waiting for something to happen, and nothing was happening at all. Except that my pasty legs were finally getting a breeze.

———

Everything that I knew about beauty as a teenager told me that my body would not be good enough. But even though I could never be truly beautiful—with a body that was graceful and toned—I could try to minimize the damage. I did this by hiding the things I thought were unsightly (not beautiful), like my braces. And I did this by controlling the things about my appearance that I could control, like my weight.

Since my diagnostician had commented on my twelve-year-old body, about how he was surprised I was "that heavy," I had gained nearly fifty pounds by my mid-teens. I had leg braces by then, too—a double whammy—so obviously I couldn't afford to also be overweight.

I lost all of the weight, and then some, by avoiding the bad foods and eating the good ones—then weighing, calculating, and adding up all of the calories even for those. I was rigorous and diligent; I had to be, if I was going to have a chance of being desirable.

When I met Josh, I hoped that he could learn to accept the parts of my body that were still not ideal. What I hadn't bargained for was that he would question the validity of my thoughts, and fundamentally not understand why I considered these parts of myself to be flaws. He thought I was beautiful, without any qualifications. No "despite" this or "in spite of" that.

I tried to dismiss away Josh and his strange ideas by telling myself that he was wired differently than other people. And while it was sweet and refreshing and all, I couldn't listen to him.

But when I did listen once and I let the world see my braces and nothing happened—it was like taking a pin out. I saw myself closer to how he did, and I let go of the rest.

———

My medical leave had turned from one to two years, and though I had been doing some volunteer work to keep my resume from going stagnant, it was time to finish my degree.

I applied to several colleges in Northern California.

One by one, I started receiving rejection letters from my top choices.

Except for one! Thankfully it only takes one, and shortly after receiving my acceptance letter my mom and I toured the campus, found the cheap Chinese food for study nights, and even found an apartment for me just off campus. The fall term was not far away, so we wasted no time finalizing all of the details—meeting my future roommates, working out the rent deposit—and getting ready to sign up for classes.

On one of our trips to the campus, after some more Chinese food, we went to one of the administration buildings and I waited in line to register for classes.

But when I reached the front of the line—gave the bored worker my name and ID number—he told me that I was coming up as a rejected applicant.

What?

That was my response to him, but of course he told me he couldn't do anything except give me a number to call.

Obviously this had been some sort of mistake, and when I called that was confirmed.

There had been an administrative error and I didn't actually have enough credits to matriculate in. I was one credit short.

My mom and I called more numbers, spoke to more bored workers and some who at least pretended to care, but the answer was the same.

They had admitted me by mistake.

I had one more rejection letter to add to the pile.

————

I was convinced that my future was over, that I would never graduate, and that this was what I got for changing my plans to accommodate my disease. I called my parents and cried on the phone—loud, ugly, uncontrolled bursts of sobbing—about how no college wanted me (and why would they? I was now both a high school and college drop-out thanks to this damn disease) and now I would never graduate or have the future I wanted.

The only school I still hadn't heard back from was UC Berkeley, and even though that would have been my first choice, I knew the likelihood of being accepted there was nil (especially after the slew of rejections). I only applied there because it was as easy as checking another box and so why not.

Even when I knew their decisions had been posted in their online portal, I didn't look. What was the point when I knew what it was going to say? I couldn't handle seeing another rejection in print.

I made the mistake of telling Josh that I had decided not to check my admissions decision. He began a relentless campaign to try to get me to check, pestering and pestering me.

After several days of this, I finally logged in to my UC Berkeley admissions account in front of him. I would show him. While I loved the opportunity to be proven right (who doesn't?), this wasn't exactly going to be my sweetest victory ("HA! I TOLD

YOU! NO ONE WANTS ME!").

As soon as I entered my log-in details and pressed *"Sign in,"* the decision letter popped up on the screen:

"Congratulations! We are pleased to tell you that you have been accepted for the Fall 2012 term at the University of California at Berkeley."

There were only two more days left to accept their offer.

13

A BODY OBSERVED

R ight before my first surgery, I'd gone online and messaged a woman from the CMT Association about volunteer opportunities. I told people that I was trying to get involved so that my resume wouldn't go stale, but I also had the secret hope that maybe through volunteering for this organization, I would discover "my people." I already knew they were *my people* since I first saw a man who walked like I did when I was fifteen.

Perhaps the worst thing about judgement is that you can feel it even when it doesn't exist. Through the CMT Association, I was finally going to be with a group of people who wouldn't look at me weird, who I could be comfortable with, and who may even have had Frankenfeet of their own. I could let them see me without fear of judgement.

When I moved to California, the woman from the CMT Association and I realized we only lived a few miles apart; she led a local support group and invited me to join. It was there that I officially joined my new tribe.

This tribe had no official induction ceremony or requirements you had to meet. I had received my membership card before birth—at the point of my genetic duplication—and if anyone questioned my legitimacy in the group, those questions disappeared as soon as I walked across the room or shook a hand.

I experienced the immediate sense of belonging that I was looking for. When out to lunches as a group, before the end of the meal all of us would inevitably be lifting up our legs above the height of the table, pulling up pant legs and showing each other our braces. It would come up for practical reasons—a question like *What type of braces do you wear?*—but I think the flagrant and occasionally comical demonstrations (holding a leg up in the air with one hand, and a half-eaten sandwich in the other) were because these were pieces of ourselves that we couldn't so easily show to other people.

What I didn't anticipate was the level of comfort people with my disease would have about commenting on my body.

It always started out so innocently, which made the comments and their sting even less expected. I might be talking to someone about our mutual symptoms, and in that conversation I would comment that my hands had gotten weaker. They'd cast their eyes down to my hands, and pulling their faces into a frown say "Yeah... I can tell."

At the end of one of the group meetings, a grey-haired man I hadn't yet met came up to me and took my hand into his. I had shared my personal story for the first time with the group, and so I took this hand-holding as a sympathetic gesture. I waited for him to introduce himself. Instead, he spoke to the woman standing beside him.

"Look, her hands are bad like yours," he said, holding my hands to her for her own inspection.

The woman murmured in agreement; then he dropped my hands and they walked away.

———

At a conference for people with CMT, I recognized someone I had befriended on Facebook. Walking up to him I said, "Hey, glad to meet you in person! How are you enjoying the conference?"

He looked me up and down and replied, "Well... my wife and I were really concerned about her and her symptoms, but now that we've come here, and I've seen you, I realize she isn't actually doing that bad.

"I hope you don't take any offense to that."

———

It is such an odd feeling to be looked at—as something strange, intriguing, different—even—especially—by your own people. I don't know that I would even know—really *know*—that I was different if so many people didn't tell me.

My parents certainly never told me. My mom never noticed, and if my dad did notice, he didn't think it was worth bringing up.

If I am still seen as something to stare at by my own people, how does that bode for my interactions with the rest of the world? What do you do when your own community says *I'm glad I'm not like you*?

———

My mom and I were walking together through an airport when I heard:

"Excuse me, do you need a wheelchair?"

It hadn't been two minutes since our last interruption (the

same question) when I saw this second employee in my peripheral vision. I looked toward him and saw concern on his face. Looking away, I said "No."

I stopped walking, forcing my mom to stop with me. Without breaking eye contact, I said aloud—to her, to myself, to whoever would listen—"I hate it when this happens." A stranger's kindness was just reminding me that I look like someone you need to be kind to. Even though I no longer needed a wheelchair, I still sure looked like someone who needed a wheelchair.

"I don't understand," she said. "Why did they think you need help?"

"Because of the way I walk."

She took this in. Rarely at a loss of words, this meant my mom must be absorbing something really difficult.

"They can really tell?" she finally asked.

"...Yeah. Why did you think the first guy stopped us?"

"I thought he was just being nice."

"No, I just obviously need help," I said, hoping that my sarcasm was thick enough.

"Does this happen often?"

"Yep."

"Wow, that would never occur to me. I don't even notice!" she laughed.

It was true. This wasn't the first time I had had to remind my mom that I am disabled.

My mother's blindness to my imperfections, to my disappointment, didn't extend to the clothes I left on the floor or the dishes in the sink. It seemed to be selective to her seeing me as someone with a disability. While she took me to my physical therapy appointments and yelled at doctors who didn't believe my complaints and told her to take me to a psychiatrist, she was never able to see the walk or my thinning wrists or the tremor in my hands. It was her blind spot.

Her blindness wasn't shared by the other people in my life.

While in a playful argument with my father as a teenager, I was in need of a way to establish my superiority. My dad taught me to never give up an argument, even if you have to make facts up.

"Yeah, well, the nurses rated me a 10 when I was born!" I told him.

"You weren't a 10," my dad said.

"What?"

"You got a 9 because you were a little jaundiced."

"Mom told me I was a 10."

"You believe her memory over mine?" he countered.

He had a point.

He could read my face, and continued. "Yeah, that's what I thought. If it makes you feel better, a nurse told me only the children of pediatricians get a 10."

It did make me feel better. Of course, he was probably making that fact up.

To this day my mom and dad disagree on this point. Mom always insists I was a 10.

———

I began summer classes at Berkeley just a few weeks after I read my acceptance letter, one of which was an introductory writing course.

Summer courses are shorter, and so meet more frequently with a heavier workload. Our professor assigned us a new writing assignment every single day. We were halfway through the term when she gave us the assignment to write about a location or a place that scared us.

I thought about the assignment on the way home, and knew immediately what it was I *should* write about. It was a place in Berkeley, and when I went there I encountered true fear.

But when I sat at my desk to write—my fingers hovering over the keyboard—I wasn't sure if I could actually put this down on paper. I hadn't told anyone about this place. About my fear. About how much it affected me every day.

I didn't know if I could turn this in, knowing it would be read by my professor. My professor who in one sentence could make an observation on the nature of Frank Gehry's fluid architecture—or the definition of a window ("What is a window but a hole in the wall?")—and in the next mention that she used to have a coke dealer on speed dial.

She dropped these details about herself—details that most people would never divulge to strangers, let alone their students—as if they were any other old fact about her past or present.

Her ability to be so comfortable with her secrets and to speak them with ease gave her an aura of confidence and power that I wanted for myself. If I were to divulge my secret, who better to divulge it to than someone who made showing yourself look so powerful?

When I started typing, the words came easily. I finished that assignment faster than any of the others, hit print, and left it in my printer until the following morning. I didn't want to have to touch or see it before then.

———

I walked into class that day early, as I always did. My reason for being early was two-fold: I hate being late and don't like to feel rushed, and by arriving early and getting seated before everyone else, none of them would see how I walked. None of them would know.

Even though I had previously conquered my fear of letting my braces be shown, I hadn't worn shorts to a single class that summer. Some fears, I discovered, need to be conquered over and over—some lessons learned more than once.

I wasn't aware of how tightly I was clutching my paper onto my way to class that morning, until I looked down at it on my desk; the upper right quadrant was slightly crumbled and moist from sweat. I thought about all of the other things I could have written about: the cliff at the edge of campus, dark closets, or any room while taking an exam.

I tried not to think about my professor reading the paper, and when I did I calmed myself by the fact that soon the term would be over and I'd never have to see her again, and if it got awkward I could always lie and say I was practicing stuff for my first novel.

———

The classroom felt empty—with its four long rows of wooden desks—when there were only seven students in the class. Each day we pulled seven desks forward into a vague attempt at a semicircle, so that we were closer to each other and to our professor who sat behind a large desk at the front of the class.

If spontaneous combustion were possible, it would have happened to me when, shortly after taking a seat, my professor said these words:

"Today I want you all to read your papers out loud to the class."

Oh. Please. God. No.

My mind was on a loop of expletives and words of terror and desperate prayers to any entity who might be listening to my thoughts. Meanwhile, the first student—a blonde-haired jock on a rowing scholarship who looked as though he had never had a problem in his life—read his paper aloud to the class.

It was about his fear of heights, and sounded more like fiction than fact.

By the time the second student started reading his paper— *also* about heights—the room had gotten ten degrees hotter. Even though my braces were still hidden underneath my jeans, I worried that in any moment all of my shields would become useless—my jeans effectively invisible. I became aware of my body in ways I hadn't since laying in the hospital bed, before I was even allowed to flex my foot in physical therapy. It was a feeling of being trapped in my body, as I felt trapped in this room. I felt the same sense of fragility that I felt after asking someone to cut into me and piece me back together, and not the sense of confidence and power I had seen in my professor.

I wished I'd written about heights.

"Bethany, why don't you go next?"

There was no other option. I felt like one million eyes were on me as I picked up my paper—even though at a max there were only fourteen—and I felt it get wet again under my sweaty fingers.

The paper felt heavier than I remembered. I looked up at my professor's face—blank as she sat waiting behind her large desk. Why, if I didn't want to be judged, had I brought my secrets into the classroom—an inherently judgmental place? Why had I asked my professor to judge and grade me on my fear—and let her invite my peers to judge me by surprise?

I looked away from all of their faces, and I read.

"If you were to ask me what my greatest fear is, I would probably give you a cliché (but not untrue) answer—something along

the lines of "failure" or "being alone." I would be too embarrassed to admit my real greatest fear—one that I must face every day, and that quickens my heartbeat at the very thought of it: my fear of crossing the street."

I didn't look up. I didn't want to see their faces. I couldn't believe I was sharing my deepest secrets with strangers. With my classmates.

But I read on.

"Most parents have to make a 'hold hands' rule to prevent their young children from running into the street. Without a developed sense of danger, kids that age really don't know any better. But I was never one of those kids."

When I was a child the divide between me and other children—healthy children—had already begun to form. I felt it all of the time, but had never been more aware of the wall between us than when reading these words. I might as well be waving a flag in front of them while shouting *I'm different than you!!*

My heart was racing faster than it ever did when crossing the street.

"I have spent years trying to prevent people from seeing the way I walk. I strategically place myself at the end of lines and the back of groups. But in the street there is no hiding. I am a spectacle. All eyes—undoubtedly—are on me. My mind can't help but wonder whether the drivers are discussing the absurdities of my gait with their companions. Or maybe they are just lamenting my slow, staggered pace. And every day I wonder if today is the day I will fall and not be able to get back up."

I wondered whether the lightbulbs were going off. Had they all already known, or at least suspected?

"There will be many streets to cross in my lifetime, both literal and metaphorical. And there will be times that I fall, or that I'm

hit, or that someone stops and stares. But with each time I successfully cross, I feel an increased sense of pride and power. If I, the girl who was once wheelchair-bound, who couldn't get around without a scooter, can cross a street by myself, I know that I can do anything."

I almost believed those words when I wrote them. I did feel pride for facing a fear every day—for crossing streets—but I didn't feel power when I reached the other side. I felt relief and fear, because the fear doesn't leave you right away—it sticks with you. It's so comforting, though, to call back to the past—to remind yourself of worse times—in order to protect yourself and convince yourself that you've been through worse and that what's happening now isn't really that bad.

But the fear still doesn't go away.

And I didn't believe I could do anything. Not really. I wouldn't have believed I could ever read this to my class.

I just had.

At the end of my paper, there was silence. I didn't dare to look up at my classmates' faces.

An eternity passed.

And then I looked up, because I had to figure out how to get back to my seat.

They were all staring at me.

The jock spoke first.

"Bethany," he said, tears in his eyes. "We are all in awe of you."

14

LOOSE CHANGE

In the days following my reveal to my class, I felt light. I had avoided being seen at all costs, and now I'd been seen at my most vulnerable. I had stood in front of my peers, with a body that was nothing like how I thought a body should be, and they had looked at that body—at me—with awe.

But why? My body was physically the same as it had always been. What had my classmates thought was going on before they heard my essay? When they saw me walk, or hold a pencil? They must have noticed. They must have seen the ways my body was different from theirs.

Were they in awe, then, when I wrote notes with visibly weak hands?

Maybe they had always seen me, noticed me and my body from a distance, and silently been in awe then, too. Maybe they hadn't noticed anything at all. Either way, it wasn't until I stood in front of them, with a story I crafted and wrote and told, that they had the permission to acknowledge my body as different from theirs. To see my struggles—different from theirs—and to be in awe. To have a genuine moment of connection.

I had been seen, and heroically.

———

A few days later when I aced a big nutritional science exam, I planned the perfect way to celebrate my deep understanding of the importance of leafy greens and flavonoid-rich vegetables: with the biggest, sloppiest, greasiest slice of pizza I'd found in Berkeley, courtesy of Arinell's pizza, a hole-in-the-wall shop next to my apartment.

Pizza at Arinell's was by now my standard celebratory practice for everything. Plus, emboldened by my recent successes, I felt like I was able to stride confidently up to the counter to order.

"Can I have a slice of the cheese, please?"

"One seventy-five."

I handed him two dollars. "Keep the change."

With a grunt of acknowledgement, he slapped the heavy slice onto a piece of wax paper and slid it across the grease-covered counter toward me.

It was a perfect transaction. Quick. Impersonal. Easy. Cheesy.

The dripping pizza in my tiny hand, I sat on one of the little red stools and thought about the answers I'd written on my nutritional science test and which ones I'd probably gotten wrong. I was no longer concerned with academic perfection, however. I knew now that perfection was unattainable. After getting 127% on a test as a high school freshman, I had learned that 100% wasn't even perfect.

My dad's reaction when I told him I got 127%?

"Why not 130%?"

The quest for perfection in my family is never ending, even as we know it's impossible.

I asked my dad once if he ever felt guilty for giving me CMT, for stacking the deck against perfection from the beginning. His response was immediate and passionate.

"*HELL* no," he said. "What about all of the great genes I gave you? The intelligence gene, the witty gene, the good looks gene? You don't get to pick and choose your genes. One or two bad ones aren't an excuse."

Eating my pizza, I pushed worries about my exam out of my mind.

I was halfway through my greasy reward when I saw a woman walk in. I clocked her to be in her sixties; she wore several layers of tattered and mismatched clothing. She looked directly at me, pizza still hanging out of my mouth, and asked, pointing at my pizza:

"How much?"

I heard a thick accent even with so few words.

She was interrupting my solo pizza reverie. I'd come for the solitude and sense of gratification afforded by secretly eating a slice that was more grease than it was pizza. Realizing that I had a viewer made me suddenly self-conscious about the grease that ringed my mouth and had even traveled up my cheek.

"One seventy-five."

She didn't respond. Instead, she sat down at the table next to mine and dumped the contents of her coin purse on the table. I watched as everyone else actively avoided looking in her direction, even as dozens of coins rolled off the table and several clattered onto the floor.

She crouched down and scooped up the scattered coins, bits of dirt and dust and tape stuck to them. She turned to the man next to her and thrust a coin in front of his face. "This good?"

He put down his pizza with a heavy sigh, and took the coin. "Nope, this is a peso."

I expected her to ask one of us to buy her a slice of pizza. Instead, without another word, she took back her peso and, with a swoop of her arm, returned the mess of coins on the table to her purse, picked up the errant coins that had fallen on the floor, and walked out.

I felt sympathy and a touch of guilt. I threw out my grease-stained wax paper and ran (well, stumbled at my top speed) after her.

I caught up with her halfway down the block.

"Hey!" I said. "Can I buy you a piece of pizza?"

She looked surprised. But then—"Yes! Pepperoni?" I nodded, and turned to head back down the street to the shop. As I turned, she grabbed me by the arm. "Let me help pay," she said.

One of the side effects of fingers that are weakened by CMT is that it is difficult for me to hold change. That's why I'd tipped the pizza guy. "No, no, I got it," I said, but it was too late. She was already pouring coins and I had no choice but to cup my hands to try and catch them.

The coins fell through my fingers like sand. We watched together as they clattered to the ground. She looked at my hands, and back up at me, and said, "I'm sorry."

She knelt down to the ground, picked her coins up again, and when she rose, this time, as she handed me the coins again, she cupped her hand underneath mine—holding my fingers together—so that the coins would not fall out.

She waited on the street while I went back in the pizza shop to get her a slice.

When I returned, she took the slice and said "Thank you." I watched as she walked away.

Most of us operate in a shared world. I know the rules of this world, like if you get sick you go to the doctor, or if you want a slice of pizza you go to the pizza place.

As my disease progressed, I also entered a different world—the world of the disabled. This world, too, has its own rules and internal logic. Those who only observe this world will never truly know what it takes to operate in it every day.

I could tell by looking at this woman's body that she was also of a different world. The mix of sympathy and relief that happened when I looked at her is the same thing that happens when people look at my body.

For so long I had been so used to being looked at in singular dimensions—as a pair of feet by my surgeon, a mystery case by my childhood physicians, a brave confusingly disabled girl by my fellow students—that this small, brief encounter was striking.

Here I was seen as someone who lacked one thing but had another. Through her physical actions, she recognized that I live in a world she doesn't. And she was able to help me in a small, specific, real way. We each brought something to each other's world. I brought pizza to hers, she brought strong hands into mine.

We shared a feeling even more powerful and validating than awe: understanding. It was without distance, or glorification, or gawking. It was, instead, an acknowledgement that we both live in worlds that most people don't know.

15

THE MEDAL

I must have been about seven years old when my mom brought up a cardboard box from the basement. She carried it upstairs and I followed close behind her, as I usually did as a child.

When she set it down, I was finally able to peer in and see what was inside. It was full of medals, the kind that someone places around your neck. I'd seen similar-looking ones on the TV when my mom was watching the Olympics.

"Whose are they?" I asked, looking in awe at the box.

"Mine," she said.

"What for?" I looked up at her now. I didn't know how my mom could possibly win *all* of those.

"Running races, mostly marathons," she said. "My dad and I ran them together."

She rummaged through the medals and pulled one out, wiping the dust off its inscription. "This was my first marathon. My time wasn't very good, but I got better."

"Did you win?" I asked.

She laughed and said no, that everyone gets a medal for finishing, but that even finishing a marathon is pretty good.

I looked down into the box. There were at least a dozen more, all tangled up in one another. Bronze and silver and gold colored discs attached to brightly-colored ribbons.

I picked up a medal from the pile and ran my tiny, chubby fingers over its bronze finish. I didn't know then that I had CMT. I didn't know that I would never win medals like Mom's. Not for marathons.

———

I used to run. I never ran a lot, and my dad tells me it didn't look much like running at all, but it *was* running. One day, not long after holding that medal, I ran for the last time. I would never run again. It wasn't an active decision, or even a passive one, it is just how my world worked. How it works for everyone: if you live long enough, everything will have its last day.

I just didn't know the end of running would come so soon.

It is only looking back now ten to fifteen years later that I begin to wonder. When did I run for the last time?

How can you possibly know that something is the last time you will ever do something? We tend to notice this only for big events. The last day of high school, for example. The last day as a single person. But running? How would you ever know?

Yet now...

Late at night...

As I type these words with only three weak, bent fingers...

I find myself thinking of running. And wishing I had run just one more time.

———

I come from a line of athletes. My mother, a long-distance runner. Her father, a born sprinter. My grandfather ran every morning until—literally—the day he died. He was entering that morning's time into his logbook when he suffered a fatal heart attack.

But that is my maternal line—the line without the gene for CMT.

Children are told that they can be whatever they want to be, if they just set their minds to it. But no one ever entertained the possibility of me being an athlete.

My mother suffered from chronic wanderlust and was easily bored. She flew glider planes before she was old enough to drive, graduated high school early, and began traveling Europe—alone—at seventeen. She lived in a castle and on a ship and had been to twenty-five countries before I was born.

And she ran marathons.

As a teenager, when I realized that I was different, I also saw the different future I would have had if I'd been born without CMT.

I imagined I would have been more like my mother. I would live a life of adventure, and I, too, would run marathons.

———

Once I was at Berkeley, I was walking farther—and without pain—than I ever had before. Against the advice of my family, I sold my wheelchair and scooter and insisted on walking everywhere. *Because now I could.*

Walking was still challenging, especially given the hilly landscape of the Berkeley campus. And there were still many streets to cross, both literally and metaphorically.

There were many things that presented a risk to my remaining vertical—such as someone looking at her phone, or a particularly strong breeze.

———

There was one day at Berkeley when I was really struggling on my way to class. It was a solid mile walk and there was a very large hill that I needed to climb on the way there.

I was about halfway up the hill when I had to stop for a minute to catch my breath. I was breathing hard and my legs were visibly shaking, even while standing still in the ninety-degree heat. It was while standing there that I noticed two guys sitting up at the top of the hill. They were looking at me.

I quickly looked away and back down at my feet, and kept on walking. But now all that I could think about was what they were thinking about me. Were they laughing with each other about the way I walk? I became, in that second, extremely aware of my unnatural gait—which was even more exaggerated by muscle fatigue. My braces were on full display since I was wearing shorts, so they knew that something was wrong. Maybe they were taking turns guessing what it was.

My head was still filled with all of the things I imagined they might be thinking or saying when I heard one of them shout to me:

"You can do it!"

I kept walking but looked up. The voice had been kind—encouraging—and belonged to a young guy in his twenties with long hair and a scruffy beard.

"Thank you!" I shouted back.

"I love you sister!" he said. (This *is* Berkeley, remember.)

"I love you too!" I yelled back.

―――

I learned through one of those for-fun at-home genetic testing kits that I have fast-twitch muscle fibers. It classified me as a "likely sprinter." At first I laughed. It felt like a cruel joke.

A lot of good that alpha-actinin-3 protein is to me now.

But then I considered what that meant. Yes, I have a gene that causes CMT. I also have some genes that are trying to make me a sprinter. Why should the gene for CMT negate all others?

The genes themselves are fighting it out.

I thought I would put them to the test and see how far I could walk.

I may have the gene for CMT, but I am still my mother's daughter.

———

I decided that I would attempt to walk seven miles and try to raise $7000 for the CMT Association.

And so I trained, each day walking a little farther than the one before. With every step I grew stronger, and I began to see my body for what it could accomplish, not just for how it could hurt me.

I was training one day by walking laps around my apartment complex, and I noticed that a construction worker was watching me. As I approached, she smiled and reached out her arm to give me a high five.

I can't straighten my fingers enough to high five, so I offered her a fist bump instead.

———

I like to talk on the phone while walking, and during another training walk around my apartment complex I was talking to my mom on my earbuds. The cord disappeared at my hip, where my phone jostled in the pocket of flowy purple workout pants that shielded my leg braces from view.

My mom and I were chatting about familial updates and drama, and how I was feeling about my upcoming walk. We could talk for hours while I walked, and often did.

"I feel like I have so much energy today," I said, before pausing to pull my phone out to check the app keeping track of my distance. "I am almost three miles in and not even tired yet!"

"Bethany, it's just amazing how far you've come," she said.

I could always count on Mom for encouragement, especially on the bad days.

But this was a good day. I was walking two hours every day, and it was finally paying off. It was getting easier. And I was training to walk seven miles. Me!

I was so enthralled by my bragging to my mom about my progress that I didn't notice the woman walking toward me from across the street until she was standing right in front of me. I figured she was looking to ask me for directions, which unfortunately for her was terribly misguided—I have a terrible sense of direction.

Sure enough, she took a step closer and said: "Hi, can I ask you something?"

"Sure!" I said. Then pausing, I spoke into the microphone attached to my earbuds, "Hey, sorry, just a sec."

The woman looked embarrassed and said, "Oh, I'm sorry, I didn't realize you were talking to someone. Never mind!"

Her cheeks were flushed, and she fidgeted with her hands while shifting her weight back and forth. I thought she might take off right there out of nervousness! I felt sorry for her. I, too, have been lost and needed to ask strangers for directions.

"No, no, it's fine!" I reassured her. "What's your question?"

"Can I pray for you?" she said.

Her question hit me like a bowling ball landing on my gut. The energy I'd been buzzing with seconds before had disappeared. I was without air and without words for a response.

I stared at her for what felt like a very long time, but was probably only one or two seconds.

"No," I said.

I have had people ask to pray for me before. I've even had people lay "healing hands" on me.

My answer has always been yes, regardless of whether I expect their prayers to create results.

But once again, this was a reminder that even when I am feeling my strongest and most able, some strangers look at me with pity. They see me as a crippled child in urgent need of divine intervention.

"Mom, I'm back."

I told her what had happened.

Her response was immediate and heartfelt.

"Oh, Bethany, I am so sorry."

That empathy and validation was all I needed. I broke into sobs and she consoled me as I walked home, beaten. She consoled me like I was once again a scared little girl climbing into bed with her after a nightmare. When I had a nightmare she would hold me, rubbing my back with one hand and stroking my hair with the other, and singing "My Favorite Things" from *The Sound of Music*.

She didn't sing to me now, or stroke my hair; she just listened.

"Is my walk that bad?" I asked her, seeking reassurance.

"It's a little different, I guess, but I don't really notice."

I took that and held onto it.

I wish that the fact I walk differently wasn't the first thing people see. With my mom, she doesn't see it at all.

———

A few days before my seven mile fundraising walk, I was sitting in the passenger seat of my Grandma Dorothy's car, door ajar. We were in the parking lot of an Applebee's, and I was busy shoving my legs into my leg braces while the middle aged man in the car parked next to ours chatted up my grandmother. Once my braces were on, I broke their conversation by telling my grandmother that I was ready. The man looked over at me and smiled. "You look good... considering," he said.

"Considering what?" I asked.

"Considering you're wearing leg braces."

I looked down at my legs, stretched out from my jean shorts. They were usually ghostly pale, hidden under long pants and jeans even on the hottest days. But for the first summer since I was a child—discovering green mashed potatoes and swinging at the park—they were sun-kissed. They were sun-kissed but they were also strong after months of walking—maybe not strong by anyone else's measurement, but they were by mine.

I smiled back and said, "I like to think I just look good. Period."

———

Originally I imagined my fundraising walk would be me and Josh walking alone in the park. Instead, my family and local CMT support group decided that they would help me to turn it into a real event. I didn't know to what extent until the morning of.

My mom arrived at my front door to pick me up and take me to the park for the walk. She was flanked by several extended family members and all of them wore matching shirts that said *Bethany's Walk to Run* on them.

I had told her that I was doing this walk—and fundraising— so that one day I might be able to run.

There were over sixty people at the designated picnic area in the park, including two local news crews. Everyone—even the reporters—was wearing a *Bethany* shirt.

I started walking laps around the 0.4 mile loop; we had calculated that I would need to complete eighteen laps around to make a total of seven miles. Many walked with me, and those who couldn't (many in attendance also had CMT) cheered me and our group on as we came around every lap. Josh held my right hand while others—family, friends, people I was meeting for the first time—took turns holding my left. I was literally being supported and held up by my community.

My mom ran marathons. I may never be able to run a marathon, or run any distance ever again, but I have learned that I am a terrible predictor of the future and so hesitate to say so definitively. Walking laps around that park on that warm August day, I wasn't running any marathon. But there is no magic in the distance of a marathon—26.2 miles—other than that it is universally recognized as a physical feat that takes rigorous training, discipline, sweat, and hopefully not—but possibly—blood and tears too.

No, I wasn't running a marathon. But I was completing a feat that no one there would have thought possible for me two years before, when I relied on a wheelchair, and the steps I did take were accompanied by pain.

My genes were fighting it out, and some of them—those sprinter genes, those genes for willpower—were finally coming out ahead. I was my mother's daughter. And I was walking seven miles.

Three hours, twenty-three minutes, and forty-seven seconds after I began, I completed the final lap for a total of 7.06 miles (according to my GPS tracker, which counted every precious step).

My mom was the first to embrace me when I reached the finish line. She held me and then, with tears rolling down her cheeks, she placed a medal around my neck.

16

APRIL FOOLS'

While attending Berkeley, I lived alone just off campus in a studio apartment; it was a super spacious 244 square feet and *all mine*. It even had two large windows with a view... of the brick walls of the buildings next door.

The floor was slanted so much that I had long since removed the wheels from my little red leather desk chair. If I didn't, as soon as I lifted my feet off the floor, I went sailing across the room. (This was very entertaining the first couple times, but the glee wore off quickly.)

Josh and I quickly agreed on a visitation routine. He lived and worked fifty miles away, which felt close because of our previous long-distance status—but that number isn't very meaningful when you factor in Silicon Valley traffic, which is legendarily horrific. (At its worst, three hours to go three miles.) Despite the distance, he visited me every weekend with rare exception. Every Friday he took a bus straight from his office to the train station, took the train to San Francisco, rode the subway across the bay to Berkeley, and then—finally—walked to my little studio apartment with the orange door: apartment number 303.

Our weekends were lazy and unexciting to outsiders due to

mutual sluggishness and possibly accelerated senescence. Outings usually consisted of eating out at one of the many wonderful and varied restaurants in Berkeley—where we first tried Tibetan and Indonesian food, and discovered that bubble tea doesn't actually have bubbles in it. The other outing, which occurred every Saturday, was a shopping trip for my groceries for the following week. Over time, there grew a mutual understanding that as long as Josh carried the groceries back for me, he could add whatever he wanted to the cart—usually a pint of ice cream.

While back at apartment 303, we worked our way through many TV series together on Josh's laptop while cuddled together on the couch, which was also my bed. In a small living space, multipurpose furniture is critical.

And on Sunday—every Sunday at 10:50 a.m.—I waved to him as he left and headed back home.

———

I was sitting at my desk—in my little red chair—when I heard a knock at my door.

Knock, knock.

I swiveled around in my chair toward the door. It was almost 9 p.m.—who would possibly be at my door at 9 p.m.? Actually, no one was ever at my door. The only visitor I ever had was Josh.

But it was Tuesday. It couldn't be Josh.

Who was at the door?

It's amazing how a door can suddenly look so much more menacing and you can go from feeling cozy in your apartment to realizing how weak and vulnerable you really are. Did my neighbor need to borrow a cup of sugar? Was I about to be murdered? Why hadn't I put pants on? Could I get away with throwing a towel around my waist? Yes if it were a neighbor, but definitely not if it were a killer. They'd warned me about Berkeley, about living alone.

Knock knock.

"Who's there?" I stammered while pulling on my pants and nearly falling over.

"Surprise pizza delivery!" said the voice behind the door.

I knew that voice. It was Josh, although it sounded like he was trying to disguise his voice (poorly).

I opened the door and saw Josh standing there—in a t-shirt and jeans, the standard uniform for a computer programmer—but no pizza.

"What are you doing here?" I asked.

"April Fools'!" he said. It *was* April 1st, but this was still a suspicious explanation—and already I was thinking, *But he didn't come up midweek for Valentine's Day... or his birthday...*

I decided to accept it. For now.

We walked the two short paces over to the couch-bed where we curled up and watched the finale of *How I Met Your Mother* together on his laptop.

———

The finale was incredibly unromantic, but it didn't seem to faze Josh. After putting his laptop away, he kneeled at the edge of the bed, stroking my face and staring into my eyes.

"Do you want to... watch something else?" I asked.

"No, I'd rather just cuddle a while longer," he said.

He stayed there, still kneeling on the floor, telling me how he loved me. "I want to spend the rest of my life with you... having days just like this... just cuddling on the couch and enjoying being with each other," he said. Then, adjusting so that he was on one knee, he added, "And in the theme of surprises..." He reached behind him and held out a small white jewelry box in front of me. Opening it, he asked, "Will you marry me?"

———

For a year or two after my surgeries, I felt like I had cheated the system. With CMT your condition is supposed to get progressively worse, but I was getting progressively *better*.

That was all well and good (and it *was* very good), but what I failed to realize is that while the oscillating saws and screws and plates and sutures allowed me to regain function and experience some muscle growth, the nerves beneath the whole system were still decaying.

Maybe I knew this logically, but I also assumed that even though the insulation of my nerves was wearing away, the nerves themselves were mostly alright. And that once a treatment is available (which there probably will be in my lifetime), everything would go back to normal. And in the meantime, I would keep getting stronger. I would keep getting better.

But eventually, that progress slowed or stopped completely, and I began to see the limits of what surgery and willpower alone could afford me.

It was at a CMT conference in Los Angeles where I finally understood the true situation. The neurologist there explained how over time as the insulation is damaged, the nerves themselves are damaged too, and they begin to die.

They *die*.

But still, if you were to ask me now, when I look into the future, at Josh and I old together... I would not see me in a wheelchair.

Because no one does.

Josh and I are both aware that a healthy future is uncertain. It is uncertain for everyone, but more so for us. It is even inevitably *un*healthy. But no one thinks that way when they are getting engaged, do they? Even we don't have those conversations, beyond the practicalities. (Maybe we should live in a location without a lot of ice and snow, or a house without a lot of stairs.) Maybe we should have those conversations, but we don't because it is uncomfortable, or depressing, or unproductive. Maybe we don't have those conversations because we have already had them silently, with ourselves. It would be ludicrous to think that Josh hasn't considered the potential futures in his own mind—Josh, the man who gave me an engagement ring with sapphires and diamonds in a prime number sequence "because it was cool."

Or maybe we don't need to have those conversations because we have already peeked behind that curtain, and lived a life where Josh *was* pushing me in a wheelchair without complaint.

He pushed me when he was twenty—before he ever told me he loved me—so I know that if I need him to again, he will.

I grew up thinking that all grandmas wore leg braces (or at least lots of them). I also grew up watching my paternal grandparents love each other; the fact that my grandma wore leg braces seemed irrelevant to that equation.

It was very relevant. It was relevant because my grandmother did change from the woman my grandfather married—a woman I know only from the black and white photo I have of them on their honeymoon, both smiling, with her on his lap and dressed in a pretty dress and black heels.

I never had high heel days, and hers, too, came to an end. Her heels were replaced with braces, walkers, canes, and wheelchairs.

That was the only grandma I knew—the one my grandpa still called his "bride" even when they were in their eighties.

How can that not be relevant to their love story and the vows they'd made over forty years before?

I also saw how, just as he cared for her, she cared for him. She cared for him by buying his clothes, continuing to cook his meals despite weakened hands, cleaning their home, handling all of the innumerable social obligations that he could never understand, and loving him even when he drove her batty and made her say "*Jim*!!"—without ever unleashing her full Irish temper.

Maybe that is what helps me to see that as Josh cares for me, I care for him too. He both shops for and carries the groceries, and I understand that he needs alone time every evening. He has learned when I need an arm or a hand for support, and I have learned when he needs me to put away my laptop so that he can lay his head on my lap. He will help me take off my shoes and my leg braces, and I make a note to remember that he prefers to sit on the left side of the couch, sleep on the right side of the bed, and sit on the right side of the car.

We care for each other.

Josh has always been caring. I have only known him for seven years, but I have sources who have known him for much longer.

His mom told me that when Josh was in fourth grade and his little sister, Sarah, was in second, they had back-to-back lunch periods at school. Every day Josh would find Sarah in her lunch line to make sure that she was okay and to give her a hug and a kiss, even though the other boys in his grade would make fun of him.

Josh in no way needs to be needed, though, and doesn't romanticize my disease.

He wouldn't say, for example, that my condition has made me a better person—the person he loves. Because there is no way we can know that is true, and he and I would both be okay with me being a slightly less good person if it meant I didn't have to needlessly suffer.

He also wouldn't say that my CMT doesn't matter.

Josh has never been *really* drunk in his entire life, but the closest he came was the wild and crazy night of his 21st birthday—and by "wild and crazy" I mean his roommates insisted he have a couple celebratory shots.

This was back when we were both going to school out in Pennsylvania and, although I couldn't be there in person on his actual birthday, we video-called after his roommates had stopped trying to get him to drink more and gone to bed.

The alcohol hadn't worn off yet, and so I took the opportunity to make a mistake I'm sure other nineteen-year-old girls have made before me: ask questions I didn't really want the answers to.

I don't know what the exact question I asked was, but it was probably something obnoxious like "Do you ever wish I didn't have CMT?"

I *do* remember the answer I got though.

"There are some times I ask myself... why am I even dating this girl... when there are so many things she can't do? But then even thinking that I feel so sad... because I can't imagine not having you in my life."

CMT is one of the "hard times" people talk about in marriage. It is the "sickness" of "in sickness and health." It isn't fun for either for us.

I wish that those things weren't already on our minds, even if they are rarely spoken. I wish that I didn't slow him down when we take walks together, even though he never tells me to hurry up. I wish I didn't see fear in his face—that is usually *always* calm—when I have trouble breathing.

Josh and I have committed to a life together, but we don't really know what that will entail—not any more than the next couple. So for now, my visions of the future are just as cheery and just as trite as the next. Right down to the white picket fence.

———

I remember asking "Are you joking?" even though I knew he wasn't joking, but it seemed like the thing to say when someone proposes on April Fools' Day. I remember crying and laughing and not being able to say anything at all. I remember reaching for the ring, and grabbing the whole box—ring still tucked safely inside—to get a closer look. I remember—finally—saying yes, but he insists the grabbing for the ring *definitely* came before the yes (it probably did).

We both knew it would be a yes, anyways.

I remember that when I grabbed the box I fumbled with it and felt it falling through my hands, but he caught it, plucked the ring out, and slid it onto my finger.

I also remember later I asked why he had chosen a diamond ring. He said, "With the amount that you fall and bump into things, I figured you needed the hardest rock they had."

EPILOGUE

I padded down the hall with my socks in hand and, stopping at the neat row of shoes—seven pairs, all with low heels—scooped up the pair with the leg braces already sticking up out of them.

Unlike Grandma, who wore stockings under hers, I wear short brightly-colored socks. Pink today, blue tomorrow, maybe purple the next. But the ritual is the same no matter the type or the color of the socks. The socks come first, each foot pulled up onto your lap to make it easier to reach. Wait, no, first you have to roll up your pant legs. Then come the socks. Once the foot is on your lap, you can roll up the sock and slowly slide it on. Then each freshly socked foot is stuffed into the shoe, and you pull the strap of the brace through the loop—just as I watched Grandma do. Then the laces are tied, and finally, after all of this is complete, the pants can be rolled back down and smoothed out over the visible lumps from the braces.

I did all of these things, just as I do every day. And, like most days, as soon as my legs were braced and ready, I was out the door and on my way to get a coffee.

It was over a year before that Josh and I were married under an oak tree in California, and nine months since we'd left our lives there to move to London, England. I really am my mother's daughter, and have her same wanderlust.

I stepped out of our flat onto the bustling streets of Notting Hill. I walked past construction workers who are ever-present in a city whose construction is unending; one was pushing a wheelbarrow full of bags of cement while several others carried large, long sheets of wood that I expertly wove around and dodged. I walked past young mums who had just dropped off their little ones at school, and exchanged smiles with one who had opted to ride her child's small orange scooter back home—because you're never too old to have fun like a child. I walked past market stands piled high with produce and specialty boutiques and a man swearing in Spanish into his mobile phone, past old English gentlemen in caps and past excited tourists pointing at the red double decker buses whizzing by. I walk over cobblestones and past buildings that make you feel like you've been transported to a Dickens novel.

———

A week before I'd walked into a clinic to see a neurologist for the first time in six years. Actually, longer, since the last time I'd seen a neurologist I'd been wheeled in.

And for the first time, I let them perform the tests my diagnostician had wanted to perform when I was twelve. The tests my grandmother had so fiercely guarded me against, begging my father on the phone to not let them hurt me, her baby.

But Grandma isn't around to protect me anymore. I opted to have the tests to give them the data they would want if I were to ever enter a clinical trial. And because I, too, wanted the data.

I have learned, through reading my charts and surgical reports and—always—asking too many questions, that there are some things best left unknown. But there is also value in being able to explain your physical world, and to have your experience in your body validated. I had heard other people with my disease relay how fast (or in this case, slow) their neurons transmitted signals compared to healthy ones, and I wanted my own numbers.

I didn't cry until the needle he jammed into my thigh. I was crying enough that it seemed to make the technician uncomfortable, and he suggested we stop the test.

"But... did you get the data?" I squeaked through tears. "Did you get all the data?"

I must have sounded hysterical, because he called in backup right after.

When I returned to the neurologist to hear my results, I asked her, "Can you tell me how slow my signals are compared to someone who is healthy?"

She looked away for a moment, and then said, "Well, I could... but we actually didn't get very many signals at all."

The cobblestones used to send me tottering, but now I walk over them with ease. It turns out, some things do get easier with practice.

Others don't. As I round the corner, I walk past the Starbucks—my old paramour from California—because it would require crossing a street. We can't overcome something every day.

Instead I stay on my block and enter my new familiar place:

Caffe Nero.

The barista recognizes me—they all do. When I reach the counter, before I can even open my mouth to order, she says, "Iced latte with soya?"

I nod affirmatively.

I've watched other customers receive and enjoy their drinks, and they always have to fetch their own straws on the other side of the cafe. Somehow, mine always comes with a straw.

And when the weather gets cold and my iced latte becomes a hot one, I know that the barista will carry it over to my table, without saying a word or my asking. I have never seen them carry anyone else's drink.

———

I like data and numbers. They tell you information. For so long, I relied on numbers—counting—to keep track of the procedures and things that were done to my feet while I wasn't awake. And I used numbers to count the steps and the miles after recovery, to measure how my body was progressing, and whether it was getting closer to the body I wanted it to be.

I never wrote a thank you card to my surgeon. Not because I wasn't thankful—I was, I am, and so deeply. My surgeon may not be a God, but he did make me walk again. I never wrote because I was waiting for the right time, when I had accomplished something incredible and then I could say: *Look, I did this because of you. Thank you.*

I looked forward to writing that thank you, about how that moment would feel.

I walked seven miles, but that wasn't good enough. It wasn't worthy of the thank you.

The next year I walked 13.1 miles—a half-marathon—but

still, that wasn't good enough.

The year after that I walked another half-marathon, and this time I shaved an hour and a half off my previous time. But still, it wasn't enough.

On this day, I know what I want to tell my surgeon—the news I waited for so long to share.

Today, I walked out my front door, I walked a block to a cafe, and I ordered a coffee.

And today, that is enough.

ACKNOWLEDGMENTS

My dad, Tom, raised me to never feel incapable. He taught me to look at everyday moments with wonder, to always question, and to find the story. Dad, thank you for giving me the courage to say: "I'm going to write a book."

My mom, Renee, sang songs to me when I had nightmares as a child, and today she continues to be a source of compassion and understanding during times of fear or self-doubt. She was also a total sharp-eyed champion during the editing process. Thank you, Mom.

My husband, Josh, has never doubted me. He has been an unbelievably patient supporter during the long writing process: reading drafts, keeping me calm when I've wanted to rip them apart, and always being Team Bethany. Josh, thank you for questioning the ways in which I see myself; I'm more grateful for you every day.

And to the three of you: thank you for graciously allowing and trusting me to share a piece of you with the world.

Thank you to my friend Elizabeth, whose thoughtful reading and feedback were a gift to me (and whose friendship likewise is).

Finally, thank you to my editor, Eva, for her incredible editorial direction and insight, for challenging me to be a more honest writer, and for teaching me to find my own voice. Most of all, for her belief in this story; I can not imagine a more perfect partner to have had throughout this journey.

To learn more about CMT or invite the
author to speak at your event, visit:
www.bethanymeloche.com

Made in the USA
Middletown, DE
21 February 2018